SUFFERING AND SOVEREIGNTY

SUFFERING AND SOVEREIGNTY

John Flavel and the Puritans
on Afflictive Providence

Brian H. Cosby

Foreword by Gerald Bray

Reformation Heritage Books
Grand Rapids, Michigan

Suffering and Sovereignty
© 2012 Brian H. Cosby

All rights reserved. No part of this book may be used or reproduced in any manner whatsoever without written permission except in the case of brief quotations embodied in critical articles and reviews. Direct your requests to the publisher at the following address:

Reformation Heritage Books
3070 29th St. SE
Grand Rapids, MI 49512
616-977-0889
orders@heritagebooks.org
www.heritagebooks.org

Printed in the United States of America
24 25 26 27 28 29/11 10 9 8 7 6 5 4

Library of Congress Cataloging-in-Publication Data

Cosby, Brian H.
 Suffering and sovereignty : John Flavel and the Puritans on afflictive providence / Brian H. Cosby ; foreword by Gerald Bray.
   pages cm
 Includes bibliographical references (pages   ).
 ISBN 978-1-60178-197-0 (pbk. : alk. paper) 1. Flavel, John, 1630?-1691. 2. Puritans—Doctrines. 3. Suffering—Religious aspects—Puritans. 4. Providence and government of God—Christianity I. Title.
 BX9339.F53C67 2012
 231'.8092—dc23
                          2012043440

Contents

Foreword... vii
Preface... x

1. Toward a Puritan Theology of Suffering.................. 1
2. Flavel on the Origin and Nature of Suffering............. 13
3. Flavel on Divine Sovereignty and Human Suffering........ 31
4. Flavel on God's Purposes in Ordaining Suffering.......... 57
5. Flavel on the Right Response to Suffering................ 95
6. The Assurance of Salvation in Flavel's Ministry to Sufferers.. 107
7. The Cessation of Suffering in Flavel's Ministry to Sufferers.. 135

Bibliography... 143
Index.. 157

To

**Aaron Little,
Derek Webber,
and J. R. Harris**

Co-laborers in the
ministry of Christ

Foreword

When the Christian gospel was first proclaimed, it went to a world that had little or no idea what might happen next. A few scientists had discovered some of the basic laws of nature, and in Babylonia there were astrologers who could predict the movements of the stars with great accuracy. But when it came to the ups and downs of ordinary human life, they were perplexed. How was it that good people often suffered in ways that were unjust and hard to bear, whereas evil men seemed to escape unharmed? What principle governed that kind of universe? Men searched the stars for wisdom, but it eluded them because our fate is not in the stars after all. Even the Jews, who knew that there was one Creator God who had made everything that exists and who kept it in being, asked themselves what the meaning of the hard life we are called to endure really was. Psalm 73 and the book of Job stand as monuments to their reflections on this subject, and they are as relevant today as they were when they were first written.

The Christian message came as a revelation that God had heard the cries of His people, that He had sent His Son into the world in order to suffer and die on their behalf, and that those who believed in Him would one day be taken to heaven, where there would be no more tears and no more suffering. But the questions the psalmist and Job asked were not specifically addressed. Jesus told His disciples that in this world they would have tribulation, but they were not to be afraid of it, because He had overcome the world (John 16:33). A Christian was expected to take up his cross and follow the Savior, counting it a privilege to be allowed to share in His sufferings (Matt. 16:24).

In the seventeenth century the Puritans knew that they had to tackle this question of suffering afresh. Their primary concern was to bring the gospel home to ordinary men and women and explain its relevance to them. The basic issues of life and death had not changed since the time of Jesus, nor have they in the centuries since. Inexplicable suffering is still with us, as is undeserved prosperity. Why God deals with His children in this way is as hard to understand now as it has ever been, and yet the pastoral needs of the church cry out for a word from the Lord.

This is what John Flavel set out to proclaim. He believed in the God of providence, who nurtured the birds and the lilies of the field but who also cared for His chosen people far more than He did for any of them (Matt. 6:25–34). He ministered in a time of civil war and paid the price of those who found themselves on the losing side, so he knew firsthand what it was to suffer. He was called to preach to men and women who had little cause to hope for a better future and good reasons for thinking that worse was yet to come. We who live in affluent, modern societies can scarcely imagine what it was like to live in fear of famine, drought, and plague. We know more about incurable illnesses, which are still with us, and probably a great deal more about psychological trauma and stress-related conditions. Circumstances may have changed somewhat, but the underlying challenge that the reality of suffering presents to the gospel message remains what it has always been.

Jesus came to proclaim good news to the poor, liberty to the captives, recovery of sight to the blind, and freedom for the oppressed—the time when the Lord would show His favor (Luke 4:18–19). Can we proclaim that message with the same integrity as He did in the synagogue at Nazareth? Or are we destined to be thrown out and rejected, as He was? Who are we to proclaim the unimaginable? And yet…

Brian Cosby is a child of God, a minister of Jesus Christ, and a servant of the gospel. The things of which he writes are not dry words on pages seldom turned for the past 350 years, but realities that are as alive for him as they were for John Flavel, the man who is his subject. Heart speaks to heart, and in this book Brian brings to life a man whom he knows as a brother in the Lord who has gone to glory. John Flavel was famous in his day and widely read for many years after his death, but fashions have changed, and today he has been largely forgotten. Even those who long to revive the Puritan heritage know little about him and wonder how they should pronounce his name! Forgotten he may be, but dead he is not. He is alive with the saints in heaven, and his words still ring with conviction and comfort to those of us who are still waiting with eager longing to join with them in the church triumphant. He speaks to our struggle and understands our sorrows, often in ways that more familiar men of the past do not.

It is my great joy and privilege to be able to commend this book and its author to a wider public. I have known Brian for many years as a student and as a pastor, and it is largely thanks to him that I have come to know John Flavel too. My prayer is that this introduction to his work will be used to bring many to a similar knowledge and understanding of one of the great men of our church and that those called to pastor today will learn from his example and be encouraged by one who suffered the loss of all things so that Christ might reign in splendor in the hearts and minds of the people committed to his care. If you are a child of God, may He do a work in you as great as the one He did in John Flavel, and may you go on your way rejoicing, knowing that in reading these pages, you have been with Jesus.

—Gerald Bray
Research Professor of Divinity
Beeson Divinity School
Samford University
Birmingham, Alabama

Preface

Immediately after catastrophic tragedies—9/11, tsunamis, floods, mass murder, hurricanes, tornadoes—television and radio programs invite religious leaders from a variety of backgrounds to explain why God would allow suffering. Some have said that these events are nothing but "natural phenomena," uncontrolled by a loving God. Others explain that these are direct judgments upon the wickedness of mankind. Still others say that these are all signs of Jesus' impending return. Why *does* God allow suffering? It's a good question.

One of the great tragedies of the American story is the loss of a biblical view of suffering, due in part to an ever-increasing belief of "entitled" health, wealth, and prosperity. We are a nation living from one pleasure high to the next—looking for the next big wave that might take us closer and closer toward the sunny sands of the American dream. The American dream not only has become something we pursue, but also something we feel we deserve. We feel entitled to life, liberty, and continual happiness. But what if the American dream is plunged into a nightmare and dashed to pieces against the rocks of suffering? Is this an "act of God"?

The effect of this trend is that the church is often like a rudderless boat without direction. The only thing we can think about is dodging the rocks of affliction up ahead or wondering why we have run into so many in the past. But this was not always the case. Various Christian cultures, communities, and movements throughout history have expressed a robust theology of suffering—one that exhibited both a right view of God's sovereignty and a right view of God's goodness—and held these two truths together in a harmonious relationship as a foundation for understanding the nature, origin, and purposes of suffering, and a right response to it. One of the clearest expressions of this can be found in the post-Reformation movement in England called Puritanism.

Many of the English Puritans living in seventeenth-century England faced various forms of suffering while also experiencing—to a greater or lesser extent—religious persecution for not conforming to the state church. Thus, much Puritan literature that has been reprinted in modern times contains theological application for the suffering believer.

John Flavel (c. 1630–1691), in particular, wrote extensively on the subject of human suffering and how it relates to divine sovereignty. He himself experienced great suffering through the loss of three wives and a son and continual persecution from state officials. Because many of his writings deal directly with the theme of suffering and because of his own experience with it, Flavel is a significant resource for understanding a Puritan theology of human suffering and divine sovereignty.

Suffering and Sovereignty seeks to examine Flavel's theology of suffering and sovereignty and how that theology translated into practical application for the suffering believer. This book started as a trimmed-down version of my PhD dissertation at Australian College of Theology and morphed into a book for the church; its aim is to capture both relevant and scholarly elements in order to form a cohesive Puritan theology of suffering.

This book seeks to build an organized structure of Flavel's theology of suffering—from its origin and nature to God's sovereignty and design for suffering to how various doctrines might comfort the afflicted. Flavel, then, serves as a representative of a Puritan theology of suffering, not only as one who exhibited all the necessary qualifications of being a Puritan but also as one who wrote extensively on the subject and faced many personal trials.

The Banner of Truth Trust's 1968 six-volume reprint edition of *The Works of John Flavel*, originally published by W. Baynes and

Son in 1820, will be used throughout unless otherwise noted. Additionally, the original spelling and punctuation of that edition will remain and, when original publication dates of seventeenth-century works are referenced, they are noted as they were originally recorded in the seventeenth century.

This study is the product of nearly six years of research, and many individuals have helped to shape this project through conversation, critique, and encouragement. I would like to especially thank Gerald Bray and John McClean for their feedback and direction. Dr. Bray in particular has been a constant resource of knowledge and support over the years in relation to this study on John Flavel. I am grateful, too, for Sinclair Ferguson, who first introduced me to Flavel and encouraged me to study him. I would also like to thank those who work in the libraries at Columbia Theological Seminary in Atlanta, Georgia; Samford University in Birmingham, Alabama; and the University of Alabama at Birmingham. They and the individuals who produce Early English Books Online (EEBO) have been tremendously helpful in finding books and articles related to this study.

I would also like to thank J. R. Harris, Christian George, Aaron Little, Norm Dunkin, Derek Webber, and my parents, who all provided continual support, feedback, and encouragement throughout the development of my research and writing. I am thankful to Adam Embry, Clifford Boone, and Nathan Parker for their correspondence on Flavel. Most of all, however, I would like to thank my wife, Ashley, for her unwavering commitment to me, her love and patience, and her desire to see this work come to fruition.

It is my hope that the content presented will both challenge and comfort the reader, in order to develop a healthier understanding of suffering and encourage the reader to give God praise in both hard times and good times—echoing the words of Job, "The LORD gave, and the LORD hath taken away; blessed be the name of the LORD" (Job 1:21).

—Brian H. Cosby

CHAPTER ONE

Toward a Puritan Theology of Suffering

Trying to make sense of suffering, affliction, and trial in light of a biblical worldview is not easy. Many questions emerge as one begins to build a theology of suffering: Is God really in control? If He is, is He morally good? Is suffering a sign of judgment, and is it truly deserved? Why does God ordain it? How should believers respond to suffering? What sources of comfort are found in Scripture for the suffering believer?

Making Sense of Suffering

Some of these questions are not only difficult to answer theologically, but difficult to understand experientially. This study seeks to present a biblical theology of suffering by turning to one of the most influential seventeenth-century Puritans, John Flavel (c. 1630–1691). Flavel, along with his Puritan contemporaries, held a unique place among the expositors of biblical doctrine. Not only did the Puritans inherit the codification and exposition of sixteenth-century Reformed theology (from Calvin, Perkins, and others), but they also had the task of developing Reformed thought by clothing it with pastoral application.[1]

The Puritans are often referred to as practical theologians, for they combined the glorious riches of biblical and systematic theology with

---

1. For an overview of the various marks of Puritans and Puritanism among historians, see Brian H. Cosby, "Toward a Definition of 'Puritan' and 'Puritanism': A Study in Puritan Historiography," *Churchman* 122, no. 4 (Winter 2008), 297–314.

the reality of life experience, like suffering. As Christians today face trials of various kinds, making sense of suffering can be achieved—at least in part—by looking back through the lens of Puritan theology to the biblical text. The Puritans were biblicists who sought to glorify God and enjoy Him forever through a life of faith and repentance. All of life, including suffering, was to be understood *coram Deo* (before the face of God) and in light of God's revealed Word, the Bible.

This book aims to present a Puritan theology of suffering by looking at one of Puritanism's greatest leaders, writers, and sufferers—John Flavel.[2] In particular, it will examine Flavel's theology of suffering within his seventeenth-century context to show his understanding of the origin and nature of suffering, how God is sovereign over suffering, why God ordains suffering, how the believer ought to respond to suffering, and how biblical doctrine can bring comfort and consolation to the believer in the midst of suffering.

Why John Flavel?

Of all of the Puritans who wrote about suffering, why pick John Flavel as a representative Puritan on the subject? It's a valid question to

---

2. For a biographical sketch of Flavel's life, see Brian H. Cosby, "John Flavel: The Lost Puritan," in *Puritan Reformed Journal* 3, no. 1 (January 2011): 113–32. Much of the biographical information in this chapter came from a variety of sources. These include Kwai Sing Chang, "John Flavel of Dartmouth, 1630–1691" (PhD diss., University of Edinburgh, 1952); John Quick (1636–1706), *Icones Sacrae Anglicane or the Lives and Deaths of Severall Eminent English Divines, Ministers of the Gospell, Pastors of Churches and Professors of Divinity in Our Owne and Foreigne Universitys* (Located in Dr. Williams Library, London, c. 1691); Clifford B. Boone, "Puritan Evangelism: Preaching for Conversion in Late Seventeenth-Century English Puritanism as Seen in the Works of John Flavel" (PhD diss., University of Wales, Lampeter, 2009); John Galpine, "The Life of Mr. John Flavell," in *Mr. John Flavell's Remains: Being Two Sermons, Composed by That Reverend and Learned Divine* (London: Printed for Tho. Cockerill, at the Three Legs in the Poultrey, 1691); Edward Windeatt, "John Flavell: A Notable Dartmouth Puritan and His Bibliography," in *Transactions of the Devonshire Association* (no. xliii, 1911): 172–89; and the anonymous "The Life of the Late Rev. Mr. John Flavel, Minister of Dartmouth," in *The Works of John Flavel* (London: W. Baynes and Son, 1820; repr., Edinburgh: Banner of Truth, 1968), 1:i–xvi.

which we provide at least four answers: (1) Flavel personally experienced severe suffering throughout his life; (2) he was very influential within his own lifetime, locally as a pastor and nationally as a writer; (3) a large portion of his writings pertain to the subject of suffering; and (4) Flavel is relatively understudied compared to other Puritan greats such as John Owen, Richard Sibbes, John Bunyan, Richard Baxter, and Thomas Watson.[3]

John Flavel was born sometime between 1627 and 1630[4] in Bromsgrove, Worcestershire. His parents were arrested and thrown

---

3. The largest recent, published study of John Flavel is J. Stephen Yuille, *The Inner Sanctum of Puritan Piety: John Flavel's Doctrine of Mystical Union with Christ* (Grand Rapids: Reformation Heritage Books, 2007). Additionally, there have been other studies on Puritanism and suffering. For example, see David W. S. Wong, "John Owen on the Suffering of Christ and the Suffering of the Church" (ThM thesis, Westminster Theological Seminary, 1990); and Erik D. Johnson, "Puritan Attitudes toward Providence and Pain: Suffering in England, 1647–1685" (MCS Thesis, Regent College, 1985). However, this later study, other than simply restating some of what the Puritans said on the subject, offers little original work, even by Johnson's own admission.

4. The actual date of his birth is unknown. Some note that he was born in 1627, such as Yuille in *The Inner Sanctum of Puritan Piety*; *Flaveliana* (Edinburgh: John Menzies, 1859); and Dewey D. Wallace Jr. in the biographical sketch in *Puritans and Puritanism in Europe and America: A Comprehensive Encyclopedia*, ed. Francis J. Bremer and Tom Webster (Santa Barbara, Calif.: ABC-CLIO, 2006), 98. But a numerical backtrack in the anonymous biographical sketch in *The Works of John Flavel* reveals that if it was not in 1628, it would have been late 1627. Others lean toward a 1630 date, such as Chang in "John Flavel of Dartmouth, 1630–1691" and James William Kelly in the *Dictionary of National Biography*. The strongest argument for the 1630 date is that Flavel's baptism is marked down as September 26, 1630, and it most likely would have fallen just days after his birth. See Kelly, "Flavell, John (*bap.* 1630, *d.* 1691)," *Oxford Dictionary of National Biography Online* (Oxford University Press, 2004), accessed February 10, 2011, http://www.oxforddnb.com/view/article/9678. Other Puritan scholars, however, lean toward the 1628 date. The best argument for the earlier date(s) is that the anonymous biographer of "Life of" in vol. 1 of Flavel's *Works* writes that he was sixty-four years old when he died, which we know was in 1691. However, a monument in Dartmouth tells us that he was sixty-one years of age when he died. If that is true, he was born in 1630. Thus there are differing pieces of seventeenth-century historical

into prison for holding an unauthorized worship meeting. While imprisoned, they caught the plague, and, although they eventually were released, both of them died shortly thereafter. Flavel's fondness for his parents, evident from his writings, made their arrest, imprisonment, and death difficult for him to bear.

After attending the University of Oxford, Flavel was ordained by presbyters in Salisbury. Tragedy struck again when his first wife, Jane, died in childbirth in 1656. Flavel writes of this loss, "The Almighty visited my tabernacle with the rod, and in one year cut off from it the root, and the branch, the tender mother, and the only son."[5] He married Elizabeth Morris soon afterward, and, as the anonymous biographer in *The Works of John Flavel* explains, was "again very happy."[6] However, Elizabeth—and later his third wife, Ann Downs—would also precede Flavel in death.[7]

In addition to these sufferings, Flavel faced the continual threat of persecution, arrest, fines, and imprisonment from state officials for being a nonconformist minister. Along with notable Puritans such as Richard Baxter, Thomas Watson, John Howe, and Thomas Manton, he was ejected from the Church of England on August 24, 1662, for nonconformity to the Act of Uniformity under Charles II. Three years later, under the Five Mile Act, he was banned from coming within five miles of Dartmouth. Reports abound of Flavel's barely escaping arrest—riding his horse into the sea or riding undercover disguised as a woman. Flavel did not write about suffering from an ivory tower, but as one who was well acquainted with a variety of afflictions.

The second reason we have chosen Flavel is that he was influential both as a local pastor in the county of Devon and nationally as a Puritan author. The royalist historian of Oxford and contemporary of Flavel, Anthony á Wood, noted that Flavel had "more

---

evidence, which makes nailing down a date very difficult. Notwithstanding, due to his baptismal record and his monument, it is probably best to take 1630 as Flavel's birth year.

5. Flavel, *A Token for Mourners*, 5:604.
6. "Life of," in *Works*, 1:v.
7. John's fourth wife, Dorothy, survived him.

disciples than ever John Owen the independent or Rich. Baxter the presbyterian."[8] Another contemporary of Flavel and one of his friends, John Galpine, once wrote that Flavel was "deservedly famous among the Writers of this Age."[9]

We also see Flavel's influence by the way his enemies viewed him. While he was in Dartmouth, some who opposed the Puritan cause carried through the town an effigy of Flavel and committed it to flames. His writings, in particular, were often sought and gathered together during protests and, afterward, burned. This happened in both England and New England.[10] In addition, Edmund Elys, a clergyman in the Church of England, wrote a letter in which he claims that there are "three Enemies of the church whose writings have made so much noise in the world, Dr. Owen, R. Baxter, & John Flavel."[11] This opposition sheds historical light on how influential Flavel really was: he, in some way, represented the Puritan element to such an extent that those who opposed the movement specifically sought to profane him and his writings.

The third reason we have chosen Flavel is that many of Flavel's writings were written directly to those who find themselves the subject of suffering. Even a cursory glance at the contents of Flavel's *Works* reveals this. Some of these include *A Token for Mourners: Or the Advice of Christ to a Distressed Mother, Bewailing the Death of Her Dear and Only Son* (1674);[12] *Preparation for Sufferings, Or the*

---

8. Anthony á Wood, Athenæ Oxonienses: *An Exact History of All the Writers and Bishops Who Have Had Their Education in the University of Oxford* (New York: Lackington, Hughes, Harding, et al., 1820), 4:323.

9. Galpine, "Life of Mr. John Flavell," 2.

10. Arnold A. Dallimore, *George Whitefield: The Life and Times of the Great Evangelist of the Eighteenth-Century Revival* (Edinburgh: Banner of Truth, 1980), 2:186; David Bogue and James Bennett, *History of Dissenters: From the Revolution to the Year 1838* (Stoke-on-Trent: Tentmaker Publications, 2000), 1:302.

11. Located in the Bodleian Library (Oxford, England: MS J. Walker e.8.32).

12. First published as *A Token for Mourners: Or, the Advice of Christ to a Distressed Mother, Bewailing the Death of Her Dear and Only Son; Wherein the Boundaries of Sorrow Are Duly Fixed, Excesses Restrained, the Common Pleas*

Best Work in the Worst Times (1681);[13] and *The Balm of the Covenant Applied to the Bleeding Wounds of Afflicted Saints* (c. 1687).[14] The theme of suffering permeates Flavel's *Works* and provides significant insight into a Puritan theology of suffering.

Finally, we have chosen Flavel because he is relatively understudied compared to many of the other Puritan greats of his day. Apart from a small handful of scholarly studies and a couple of isolated publications, the field remains wide open to continued research into Flavel's life and theology. For these reasons, Flavel is a most appropriate representative through which to gain a greater understanding of a Puritan theology of suffering.

Counterinterpretations of Flavel

Before we look at the nature and origin of suffering within Flavel's theology in light of his historical context, it is important to note that this study makes some fundamental propositions that run counter to what others have written and published concerning

---

Answered, and Divers Rules for the Support of Gods Afflicted Ones Prescribed. By J. F., Preacher of the Gospel of Christ at *Dartmouth* in *Devon* (Turks-head in Cornhill, over against the Royal Exchange, 1674). It is interesting that Flavel accuses humanity of causing "excessive sorrows" by idolizing the temporal and fleeting things of this world, including other human beings (i.e., "loved ones"). *The Balm of the Covenant*, 6:84.

13. First published as *Preparation for Sufferings: Or, the Best Work in the Worst Times; Wherein the Necessity, Excellency, and Means of Our Readiness for Sufferings Are Evinced and Prescribed; Our Call to Suffering Cleared, and the Great Unreadiness of Many Profesours Bewailed. By John Flavel, Minister of Christ in Devon* (London: Printed for Robert Boulter at the Turks-head in Cornhil, 1681).

14. The first edition's publication date is unknown. The second edition is *The Balm of the Covenant Applied to the Bleeding Wounds of Afflicted Saints: First Composed for the Relief of a Pious and Worthy Family, Mourning over the Deaths of Their Hopeful Children; And Now Made Publick for the Support of All Christians, Sorrowing on the Same or Any Other Account. To Which Is Added, A Sermon Preached for the Funeral of That Excellent and Religious Gentleman John Upton of Lupton esq; by John Flavell, Preacher of the Gospel at Dartmouth in Devon*, 2nd ed. (London: Printed for J. Harris, at the Harrow against the Church in the Poultrey, 1688).

Flavel's theology. Although these will be addressed later on, a brief mention of two counterinterpretations is in order. The first is a PhD dissertation by the late Kwai Sing Chang, titled "John Flavel of Dartmouth, 1630–1691."[15] The second is a book by Ann Thompson, titled *The Art of Suffering and the Impact of Seventeenth-Century Anti-Providential Thought*.[16]

Kwai Sing Chang's dissertation remains the only full-length biography of Flavel available, although it is unpublished. According to Chang, there were three major strands of Puritan theology in seventeenth-century England. First, some Puritans held to a "strict Calvinism," and the chief representative of this view was John Owen (1616–1683).[17] This strand was a rearticulation of Calvin's theology—encompassing everything from Calvin's understanding of revelation to the knowledge of God and man to soteriology.[18] Chang sees Owen's "strict Calvinism" as being in step with both

---

15. Chang, "John Flavel of Dartmouth."
16. Ann Thompson, *The Art of Suffering and the Impact of Seventeenth-Century Anti-Providential Thought* (Burlington, Vt.: Ashgate, 2003).
17. Chang, "John Flavel of Dartmouth," 67. For some academic studies on the life and theology of John Owen, see Dewey D. Wallace, "The Life and Thought of John Owen to 1660: A Study of the Significance of Calvinist Theology in English Puritanism" (PhD diss., Princeton University, 1965); Don Marvin Everson, "The Puritan Theology of John Owen" (ThD diss., The Southern Baptist Theological Seminary, 1959); David Wai-Sing Wong, "The Covenant Theology of John Owen" (PhD diss., Westminster Theological Seminary, 1998); Godfrey Noel Vose, "Profile of a Puritan: John Owen" (PhD diss., State University of Iowa, 1963); and Sinclair Ferguson, "The Doctrine of the Christian Life in the Teaching of Dr John Owen" (PhD diss., The University of Aberdeen, 1979).
18. For a comparative study of Owen and Calvin, see Randall Craig Gleason, "John Calvin and John Owen: A Comparison of Their Teaching on Mortification" (ThD diss., Dallas Theological Seminary, 1992). For some excellent studies on Calvin's life and theology, see Bruce Gordon, *Calvin* (New Haven: Yale University Press, 2011); Ford Lewis Battles, *Interpreting John Calvin*, ed. Robert Benedetto (Grand Rapids: Baker, 1996); T. H. L. Parker, *Calvin: A Biography* (Louisville, Ky.: Westminster John Knox Press, 2007); and David W. Hall and Peter A. Lillback, eds., *Theological Guide to Calvin's Institutes* (Phillipsburg, N.J.: P&R, 2008). For a good resource on Reformation theology

Calvin's *Institutes of the Christian Religion* as well as the Westminster Confession of Faith. The second strand that Chang identifies is Arminianism, which "attracted more Anglicans than Puritans" during Flavel's lifetime.[19] He argues that, while its prominence lay hidden during the Commonwealth and Protectorate, it reappeared with the Restoration and found sympathy with Puritans like John Goodwin (1594–1665) and John Howe (1630–1705). The third strand is "Baxterianism,"[20] which took a moderate position on church order and theology between the Calvinist and Arminian positions. Chang thus summarizes Baxter's thesis: "In things necessary, unity; in things doubtful, liberty; in all things, charity."[21]

So where does Flavel's theology "fit"? Chang argues that Flavel's theology "stood half way between Owen and Baxter."[22] In other words, Flavel—as demonstrated in his writings and sermons—can be placed as a moderate Calvinist. But is Chang accurate in his analysis? It is beyond the scope and purpose of this study to examine Flavel's theology in depth. Notwithstanding, this study contends that Flavel was in much greater agreement with what Chang sees as "strict Calvinism" (whether or not that phrase in itself is a proper designation of Owen's theology).[23] Not only does

---

in general, see Timothy George, *Theology of the Reformers* (Nashville: Broadman & Holman, 1988).

19. Chang, "John Flavel of Dartmouth," 68.

20. Taken from the theology of Richard Baxter (1615–1691). For an excellent study of Richard Baxter, see James I. Packer, "The Redemption and Restoration of Man in the Thought of Richard Baxter: A Study in Puritan Theology" (DPhil diss., Oxford University, 1954).

21. Chang, "John Flavel of Dartmouth," 69. The original source of this phrase, from the Latin *In necessariis unitas, in dubiis libertas, in omnibus caritas*, may be attributed to Marco Antonio de Dominis (1560–1624), Dalmatian archbishop-turned-apostate, in his *De Republica Ecclesiastica Libri X* (London, 1617), 1.4.8. See H. J. M. Nellen, "De zinspreuk 'In necessariis unitas, in non necessariis libertas, in utrisque caritas,'" *Nederlands archief voor kerkgeschidenis* 79, no. 1 (1999): 99–106.

22. Chang, "John Flavel of Dartmouth," 69.

23. Much of Yuille's *Inner Sanctum*, for example, attempts to show the continuity between Calvin and Flavel.

Flavel's theology agree with the Westminster Standards, but he also may be identified as a Calvinist with little or no leaning toward the moderate position of what Chang calls "Baxterianism."

In addition, while Chang finds "no consistent, definite and exhaustive system of doctrine [in Flavel],"[24] this study disagrees and finds that Flavel's theology was not only consistent but also definite, in that he was an heir and expositor of the Westminster Standards. It is true that Flavel believed himself to be a pastor and preacher, but he was a pastor-theologian. While he draws many practical applications throughout his writings, he also presents meticulous theology. This fact can be seen, for example, by his straightforward and systematic exposition of the Westminster Shorter Catechism.

The second counterinterpretative work on Flavel—at least with regard to his understanding of divine sovereignty and how one ought to respond to suffering—is *The Art of Suffering* by Ann Thompson. These two topics will be examined in depth later on, but they need some comment here at the outset.

Thompson seems to suggest that Flavel employed a deistic understanding of a "clockwork universe" with reference to God's sovereignty. Thompson bases her argument on Flavel's use of the phrase "natural causes," quoting from Flavel's *Divine Conduct*, where Flavel speaks of how God delivers His people "against the course of natural causes" and that there exists a "suspension" in these causes by God's sovereign hand.[25] While Flavel certainly employs these terms, Thompson misreads Flavel's theology of the use of secondary causes. Indeed, in the very next paragraphs and pages in *Divine Conduct* (from which Thompson quotes Flavel's view of natural causes), Flavel explains that God governs even the intimate details of these "natural causes" to His own ends.[26] Or, to put it negatively, the day-to-day events, storms, and actions of people cannot be "wholly swayed by the course of nature."[27] While "reason lays

---

24. Chang, "John Flavel of Dartmouth," 69.
25. Thompson, *Art of Suffering*, 9. Cf. Flavel, *Divine Conduct*, 4:351.
26. Flavel, *Divine Conduct*, 4:353.
27. Flavel, *Divine Conduct*, 4:354.

[these events] according to the rules of nature; providence crosses its hands…and orders quite contrary issues and events."[28] Contrary to Thompson, then, this study contends that Flavel did not hold to such an understanding of God's control, creation, or the use of "secondary causes."

The second major disagreement between the conclusions of this study and those of Thompson's book lies in the area of how the Christian was rightly to respond to suffering—what Thompson calls "the art of suffering." While we will examine this closely in chapter 5, we may summarize the disagreement here.

According to Thompson, there was a difference between the way the pre-1640s Puritan responded to suffering and the way the post-1640s Puritan responded to suffering. The pre-1640s approach is what Thompson calls the "voluntaristic art of suffering," which goes beyond merely coping with affliction to trying to find ways in which to grow from affliction. She writes, "If the art of suffering up to the 1640s teaches the sufferer both how to 'cope with' and how to 'grow from' his affliction, the art of suffering in the second part of the seventeenth century teaches him only how to 'cope.'"[29] In pre-1640s England, Thompson argues, the Puritan was to "embrace the promises made in the Word" and, therefore, reap some spiritual benefits of affliction—from the text of Scripture into his or her real-time context of suffering.[30] In post-1640s England, however, the art of suffering "is not divided into directions for the time before affliction comes and directions for the actual time of affliction."[31] In other words, Thompson contends that the pre-1640s mindset sought spiritual benefit from suffering while the post-1640s mindset sought merely a contented state of mind. The pre-1640s thought was to see spiritual directions put into practice, while the post-1640s thought was to simply listen and assent to the Puritan writer.[32]

---

28. Flavel, *Divine Conduct*, 4:354.
29. Thompson, *Art of Suffering*, 12.
30. Thompson, *Art of Suffering*, 85.
31. Thompson, *Art of Suffering*, 85.
32. Thompson, *Art of Suffering*, 88.

One of the primary reasons for this change in the response to suffering, according to Thompson, was that the seventeenth century witnessed an increase of antiprovidential thought as the century progressed. The "doctrine of the profit of affliction" came under attack toward the end of the seventeenth century at a popular level.[33]

In her final analysis, Thompson sees the post-1640s Puritan's "art of suffering" as lacking and internally incoherent, since the writer is not free to find contentment because he or she is not encouraged to pursue spiritual benefit or profitable use from his or her suffering. While such a proposition might be true of other Puritans, this study contends that Flavel's theology of suffering and sovereignty does not validate Thompson's thesis. Not only does Flavel hold to a strong view of God's sovereignty as displayed in temporal providence, but he also presents a variety of ways in which his reader is to make "profitable" use of his or her affliction.

Methodological Approach to Flavel's Theology of Suffering

This book is organized into categories of Flavel's theology of suffering. It should be emphasized that these elements were not forced onto Flavel's thought; rather, they were derived from his thought. This is an important distinction. As a systematic theology seeks to identify theological themes from Scripture and organize them in a helpful way, so also this study has sought to identify those themes related to human suffering and divine sovereignty and organize them in such a way as to organically build a theology of suffering from Flavel's writings. These elements, drawn from Flavel's *Works*, have been codified into five general categories. The first element is Flavel's understanding of the origin and nature of suffering. Some of the questions addressed include the following: Where did suffering come from, and what does it look like? Is it chiefly internal

---

33. There came to be certain "popular" objections to providential thought, particularly, the seemingly inequitable distribution of good and ill or the inequitable treatment of the wicked and the good. See Thompson, *Art of Suffering*, 8–9.

or external? What was Flavel's context of suffering in seventeenth-century England?

The second category seeks to answer one of the popular charges against God when tragedy strikes: namely, that God is not in complete control. Some of the questions answered under this category include these: Is God sovereign over suffering? How is God's sovereignty expressed or "displayed" in time and space? Is suffering considered "evil," and, if so, is God the author of evil?

The third category, drawn from Flavel's writings, seeks to address the experiential "meat" of a Puritan theology of suffering: Why does God ordain it? Why would God not only allow suffering but also ordain it from all eternity and providentially bring it to fruition in time and space? What is the purpose of suffering for the believer and for the unbeliever, respectively?

The fourth category seeks to examine how the believer should respond to suffering. It is here that Thompson's thesis will be addressed. Are there sinful ways to respond? What are the appropriate responses to suffering, and how might the Christian prepare for such responses?

The final element is Flavel's understanding of how biblical doctrine brings comfort and consolation to the suffering believer. In this category, it will be shown how Flavel sought to minister to the afflicted saint, especially with the use of covenant theology and eschatological hope.

The method, then, is inductive rather than deductive. Ultimately, these elements are woven together so as to present a Puritan theology of suffering drawn from Flavel's writings.

CHAPTER TWO

Flavel on the Origin and Nature of Suffering

Richard Rogers (1551–1618), a priest in the Church of England with nonconformist leanings, wrote a book titled *Seven Treatises*, which provided theological and practical instruction for living a godly life.¹ In it, he describes the general nature and types of suffering:

> By Troubles we do not onely meane great & vnwonted losses, long sicknesses, persecutions, and such like: but those also which fall out verie oft and commonly, as vnkindnesse and discourtesie in neighbours; vnthriftinesse, vnrulinesse and disobedience in children; vnfaithfulnesse and negligence in seruants; discommodities and harmes in family matters; with such like: all which to beare, without vnquietnesse, impatience and vnsetling our selues out of the Christian course, must be thought no meane nor smal gift of God…. It is a great point of wisedome, to learne of God, thus to beare our trials and troubles, that first we commit the ordering and disposing of them to him.²

---

1. Richard Rogers, *Seven Treatises Containing Such Direction As Is Gathered out of the Holie Scriptures, Leading and Guiding to True Happines, Both in This Life, and in the Life to Come: And May Be Called the Practise of Christianitie. Profitable for All Such As Heartily Desire the Same: In the Which, More Particularly True Christians May Learne How to Leade a Godly and Comfortable Life Every Day. Penned by Richard Rogers, Preacher of the Word of God at Wethersfield in Essex* (London, 1603).

2. Rogers, *Seven Treatises*, 394–95.

Suffering in Stuart England

Sufferings, both small and great, bore upon individual consciences and social communities during the seventeenth century. Events such as the Great Plague (1665), the Great Fire of London (1666), and continual struggles from poverty and persecution caused many to turn to the writing minister for answers, comfort, and hope.

Independents, Puritans, and conformists alike wrote of a variety of sufferings, both physical and spiritual. Independent minister Jeremiah Burroughs (c. 1601–1646) writes in *The Rare Jewel of Christian Contentment*:

> God doth give leave to his people to be sensible of what they suffer: Christ doth not say, Do not count that a crosse which is a crosse, but take up your crosse daily. As it is in the body natural, if the body takes physick and is not able to bear it but presently vomits it up, or if it be not at all sensible, if it stir not the body; either of these waies the physick doth no good, but argues the body much distempered and will hardly be cured. So it is with the spirits of men under afflictions.[3]

Conformist clergyman Richard Kidder (1634–1703),[4] in *The Christian Sufferer Supported*, writes of the close connection between the sufferings and evils endured in this life and the presence of sin. He also writes about the various "evils" people endure. He explains:

> Though many of the evils of this life, which we daily complain of, are Phantastick and imaginary, as our happiness in this world generally is; And many others, under which we

---

3. Jeremiah Burroughs, *The Rare Jewel of Christian Contentment wherein Is Shewed, I. What Contentment Is, II. The Holy Art or Mystery of It, III. Several Lessons That Christ Teacheth, to Work the Heart to Contentment, IV. The Excellencies of It, V. The Evils of Murmuring, VII. The Aggravations of the Sin of Murmuring*. (London: Printed for Peter Cole at the Printing-Press in Cornhil, near the Royall Exchange, 1649), 5.

4. William Marshall notes that Kidder had leanings toward Presbyterianism, but ultimately decided to stay within the Church of England. See William Marshall, "Kidder, Richard (*bap.* 1634, *d.* 1703)," *Oxford Dictionary of National Biography* (Oxford: Oxford University Press, 2004).

are uneasie are intirely owing to our own folly and the just fruit of our wicked lives.... Many are the evils to which we are incident, and which therefore we may justly expect: Such are Reproach and Poverty, Sickness and Pain, Oppression and Violence, Sorrow for the Death of our Friends, and the Dread and the Fear of our own. There are many in the world whose misery is great upon them and who are perpetually bowed down with some or more of these evils.[5]

Similarly, conformist clergyman Richard Allestree (c. 1621–1681), in *The Art of Patience under All Afflictions*,[6] writes of how the reader should respond to sufferings of sickness, affliction of conscience, loss of reputation, "publik calamities," loss of friends, poverty, confinement, exile, blindness and deafness, spiritual conflicts, or sterility with patience, meekness, and humility. External afflictions, internal sufferings, spiritual conflicts, persecutions, and social injustices all fall into the understanding of suffering in Stuart England.

Persecution, in particular, has become a popular topic of early-modern historical research over the last fifty years, especially as it relates to the nonconformist and dissenting communities.[7]

---

5. Richard Kidder, *The Christian Sufferer Supported, Or, A Discourse concerning the Grounds of Christian Fortitude, Shewing at Once That the Sufferings of Good Men Are Not Inconsistent with God's Special Providence: As Also the Several Supports Which Our Religion Affords Them under Their Sufferings, and Particularly against the Fear of a Violent Death.* (London: Printed for W. Kettilby at the Bishops Head in St. Paul's Church-Yard, 1680), 3–4.

6. Originally published as Richard Allestree, *The Art of Patience under All Afflictions: An Appendix to the Art of Contentment.* (London: Printed for W. Cademan in the Lower-Walk of the New Exchange, in the Strands, 1684).

7. For a sampling of some of these, see John Coffey, *Persecution and Toleration in Protestant England, 1558–1689* (Harlow, UK: Pearson Education Ltd., 2000); Alexandra Walsham, *Charitable Hatred: Tolerance and Intolerance in England, 1500–1700* (Manchester: Manchester University Press, 2006); Gerald R. Cragg, *Puritanism in the Period of the Great Persecution, 1660–1688* (Cambridge: Cambridge University Press, 1957); Mark Goldie, "The Search for Religious Liberty, 1640–1690," in *The Oxford Illustrated History of Tudor & Stuart Britain*, ed. John Morrill (Oxford: Oxford University Press, 1996); Ole Peter Grell, Jonathan I. Israel, and Nicholas Tyacke, eds., *From Persecution to*

According to historian John Spurr, "Persecution ranged from minor harassment, through disruption and rough handling by constables, soldiers or mob, personal injury and wanton destruction, to mass imprisonment."[8] Gerald Cragg has noted that, during the Restoration period, "persecution of nonconformists was the official policy of England's rulers."[9] From the rise of Puritanism in Elizabethan England to the outbreak of civil war in the 1640s, and through the Restoration period, persecution ebbed and flowed—not so much with changing monarchies, but as the enforcement of monarchial policies directed against dissenters.

The Origin of Suffering

Flavel believed that the suffering seen and experienced in this world and in the world to come is directly related to the presence of sin. Thus Flavel's understanding of the origin of suffering cannot be separated from his understanding of the fall of Adam in the garden and the effects of that fall upon the rest of humanity.[10] Flavel believed that Adam and Eve were created with intrinsic freedom of the will, but they abused that liberty and transgressed God's commandment not to eat of the tree of the knowledge of good and evil.[11] Through the sin of humanity's representative head, Adam, death "passed upon all men, for that all have sinned."[12] This happened, Flavel explains, "not by inclining him to abuse it; but by withholding that further grace which he was no way obliged to continue to him."[13]

Toleration: The Glorious Revolution and Religion in England (Oxford: Oxford University Press, 1991); W. J. Sheils, *Persecution and Toleration* (London: Blackwell Publishers, 1984); Henry Kamen, *The Rise of Toleration* (London: Littlehampton Book Services, 1967).

    8. John Spurr, *English Puritanism, 1603–1689* (London: Macmillan Press, 1998), 141.
    9. Cragg, *Puritanism in the Period of the Great Persecution*, 248.
    10. Cf. Gen. 3.
    11. Cf. Gen. 2:17. Flavel, *Exposition of the Assembly's Catechism*, 6:167, 169–71.
    12. Flavel, *Exposition of the Assembly's Catechism*, 6:167.
    13. Flavel, *Exposition of the Assembly's Catechism*, 6:168.

The effect of Adam's sin is that he and all of his posterity fell under the wrath and condemnation of God. The payment for sin was death, and Adam was barred from the "tree of life."[14] All humans, by necessity of their own nature, transgress God's commandments and laws. Other effects of the fall of Adam include the "loss of God's image," "curse on the creation," "expulsion from paradise," and "death both of body and soul."[15] Post-fall human nature, then, is wholly corrupted, or totally depraved of all goodness, righteousness, and holiness.[16]

Suffering, too, comes as an effect of sin, brought into existence by the disobedience of humanity's federal head, Adam. In Flavel's *Navigation Spiritualized* (1664),[17] he speaks of suffering and affliction as the "fruit of sin." He writes:

> Afflictions in themselves are evil, Amos ii. 6. very bitter and unpleasant. See Heb. xii. 11. Yet not morally and intrinsically evil, as sin is; for if so, the holy God would never own it for his own act as he doth, Mic. iii. 2. but always disclaimeth sin, James i. 3. Besides, if it were so evil, it could, in no case or respect, be the object of our election and desire, as in some cases it ought to be, Heb. xi. 25. but it is evil, as it is *the fruit of sin*, and grievous unto sense, Heb. xii. 11.[18]

---

14. Cf. Gen. 3:22.

15. Flavel, *Exposition of the Assembly's Catechism*, 6:170. Death, even as a curse of the fall, occurs only by the sovereign will of God. Flavel writes, "The special limit [of life] is that proportion of time, which God, by his own counsel and will hath allotted to every individual person; and it is only known to us by the event." *Token for Mourners*, 5:630.

16. Flavel, *Exposition of the Assembly's Catechism*, 6:170.

17. First published as *A New Compass for Seamen Consisting of Thirty-Two Points of Pleasant Observations, Profitable Applications, and Serious Reflections, All Concluded with So Many Spiritual Poems, Directing Them to Stear Their True Course to Heaven, and to Avoid the Dangerous Rocks on Either Side: Containing Many Things of Singular Use for All Christians, Especially for Such As Go down into the Sea, and Do Business in the Great Waters* (London: Printed for the Author, sold by Rich. Tomlins, 1664).

18. Flavel, *Navigation Spiritualized*, 5:251, emphasis added.

Flavel, then, held to a view of affliction as evil only in the sense that it is "bitter," "unpleasant," and "grievous." This view understood affliction not as intrinsically or morally evil, but as the "fruit of sin," which is one of the effects of the presence of sin in this world. However, while suffering comes as the "fruit of sin," it nevertheless comes by way of God's eternal decree. Flavel taught that one of the "instructions from God's decrees" is that "God's hand is to be acknowledged in the greatest afflictions that befal us."[19]

Flavel's understanding of suffering—being the "fruit of sin"—is similar to his understanding that suffering is the "curse" of the fall.[20] It is simply another vantage point for viewing the same reality: suffering exists as both a fruit of sin and a curse of the fall. Flavel writes, "There is *radically* all the misery, anguish, and trouble in the world in our corrupt natures. As the spark lies close hid in the coals, so doth misery in sin; every sin draws a rod after it."[21] Indeed, "sin... first brought afflictions into the world."[22] Or, to put it another way, "Sin is the cause and inlet of affliction and sorrow" and yet "providence hath ordered it all along your way."[23]

That suffering—even as an "evil"—comes as an effect of sin is, therefore, consistent with Flavel's understanding of the righteousness of God. In answering the question, "What is the goodness of God?" Flavel writes, "It is an essential property of his nature, whereby he is absolutely and perfectly good in himself, and the fountain of all communicated goodness to the creature."[24] God manifests His goodness "in the creation and government of the world."[25] This is Flavel's understanding of God calling His creation "good."[26]

---

19. Flavel, *Exposition of the Assembly's Catechism*, 6:161. This can also be seen where Flavel writes, "So men, after they have been denuded and blasted by Providence, they begin after a while to flourish again." *Navigation Spiritualized*, 5:259.
20. Flavel, *Navigation Spiritualized*, 5:218.
21. Flavel, *Navigation Spiritualized*, 5:218.
22. Flavel, *Navigation Spiritualized*, 5:253.
23. Flavel, *Divine Conduct*, 4:422.
24. Flavel, *Exposition of the Assembly's Catechism*, 6:155.
25. Flavel, *Exposition of the Assembly's Catechism*, 6:155.
26. Cf. Gen. 1:4, 10, 12, 18, 21, 25, 31.

Interestingly, Flavel anticipates that suffering might be used as grounds for objecting to God's goodness. It is important, at this juncture, to understand that Flavel believed the suffering experienced by unbelieving reprobates (the "wicked") to be God's judgment. Conversely, he believed the suffering experienced by the elect (the "saints") to be fatherly discipline. Flavel poses the objection: "But are not the judgments of God on the wicked, and his affliction on the saints, impeachments of his goodness?" Answer: "No; it is the property of goodness to hate and punish evil in the impenitent." But, "the affliction of the saints flow from his goodness, and end in their true and eternal good."[27] In other words, the goodness of God remains unstained by the presence of suffering among humanity even while He remains sovereign over that suffering.

With this view of the origin of suffering as an effect of sin, and upholding the goodness and sovereignty of God, Flavel's theology remains consistent with that of his Puritan contemporaries.[28] The origin of suffering is connected to the fall and the curse in Genesis 3. But the entrance of suffering came only as part of God's eternal decree. Clearly, then, Flavel understood God to be the author of suffering, but not the author of sin. As John Bunyan, Flavel's contemporary, once noted, "As it is appointed (who, when, where, what kind, and) for what truth by the will of God, this and that Saint should suffer: so also it is appointed by *whose hand* this or that man shall suffer for this or that truth."[29]

The miseries, curses, and evils committed by men and women upon other men and women are the direct effects of both original and actual sin. All humanity has a natural "aversion and enmity to that which is good" because "sin abides in the whole man, in every part of man, both soul and body."[30] Therefore, even the "miseries we

---

27. Flavel, *Exposition of the Assembly's Catechism*, 6:156.
28. Some of these include Richard Sibbes, Thomas Watson, John Owen, Thomas Case, Stephen Charnock, and John Bunyan.
29. John Bunyan, *The Miscellaneous Works of John Bunyan*, ed. Roger Sharrock and Owen C. Watkins (Oxford: Oxford University Press, 1988), 10:69.
30. Flavel, *Exposition of the Assembly's Catechism*, 6:172–73.

see on our children, and their death" are directly attributable to the presence and reality of sin.[31] Because of the fall of Adam, various trials and miseries entered this world; for the unregenerate, the world to come will also be full of them.[32] All of these afflictions, however, do not happen apart from the sovereign and providential governing of God. We may summarize Flavel's understanding of the origin of suffering in this way: While the eternal "origin" of affliction is placed in the decretal will of God, the fruition of it entered the world through Adam's fall into sin and remains so because he was humanity's federal head. So what did Flavel believe to be the "miseries" in this life and in the world to come?

External and Internal Sufferings

Flavel understood the greatest suffering to be internal rather than external. While external afflictions certainly are difficult to bear, internal grief, sorrow, and despair are greater. But more than this, as we shall examine in the next section, Flavel understands certain spiritual sufferings to be the greatest trials of all. Therefore, it is helpful to divide Flavel's view of suffering into three categories: external, internal, and spiritual.[33]

As far as the external sufferings are concerned, Flavel argues that the miseries of this life include "sickness, pain, poverty on the body; fear, trouble, sorrow on the mind, and at last death itself."[34] While this list includes both external and internal sufferings, we

---

31. Flavel, *Exposition of the Assembly's Catechism*, 6:173.
32. Flavel, *Exposition of the Assembly's Catechism*, 6:174.
33. While we may divide types of suffering into these three general categories, Flavel often links the last two together. For example, he asks his reader, "Are your afflictions more spiritual and inward?" He then asks the follow-up question, "Or are your afflictions outward and inward together; an afflicted soul in an afflicted body?" *Fountain of Life*, 1:365. Flavel's differentiation between internal and external sufferings is seen clearly when he writes, "It is a sad case when inward and outward troubles meet together." *Preparation for Sufferings*, 6:75. He also says the Bible "must be applied for our comfort in all inward and outward troubles." *Exposition of the Assembly's Catechism*, 6:274.
34. Flavel, *Exposition of the Assembly's Catechism*, 6:174.

surmise that Flavel held an ordinary understanding of external sufferings: those things that bring pain and discomfort to the physical body as well as those things that prompt and cause internal distress. Flavel addresses the issue of "external pains, and outward afflictions." What can they do? They can "waste and wear out the strongest bodies."[35] While these sufferings harm the body, they do not directly harm the soul.

One of the chief external sufferings—something that Flavel's *Works* treat extensively—is suffering brought about by religious persecution. He writes, "Though millions of precious saints have shed their blood for Christ, whose souls are now crying under the altar, *How long, Lord! How long!* yet there are many more coming on behind in the same path of persecution, and much Christian blood must yet be shed, before the mystery of God be finished.... Thus you see to what grievous sufferings the merciful God hath sometimes called his dearest people."[36] By physical persecution, Flavel means— in agreement with Hebrews 11—that the saints of old "were tortured, they were sawn asunder, were tempted, were slain with the sword, they wandered about in sheep-skins and goat-skins, being afflicted, destitute, tormented," and so on.[37] Other types of physical sufferings include those inflicted by harmful animals, whips, drowning in a sinking ship, scorpions, deformities, bodily flaws, bodily aches, disease, and the pains of dying.[38]

It is important to emphasize one point again: these external sufferings often bring about internal sufferings, which, according to Flavel, are far greater.[39] While "outward afflictions do but break the

---

35. Flavel, *Fountain of Life*, 1:424.
36. Flavel, *Preparation for Sufferings*, 6:9.
37. Quoted in Flavel, *Preparation for Sufferings*, 6:8.
38. Flavel, *Navigation Spiritualized*, 5:218, 220; *Seaman's Companion*, 5:342.
39. It should be noted, however, that the joining together of the outward and inward sufferings is more difficult than just taken one at a time. Flavel writes, "When outward bodily pains shall meet with inward spiritual troubles, and both in extremity shall come in one day; how soon must the firmest body fail and waste away like a candle lighted at both ends?" *Fountain of Life*,

skin, [spiritual affliction] touches the *quick*."⁴⁰ The death of a loved one—what Flavel refers to as "the greatest of earthly sorrows"—is so difficult precisely because it is a "deep and penetrating...grief."⁴¹ In fact, most everything Flavel writes with regard to suffering, he writes to counsel and help alleviate internal and spiritual pain, not physical pain. A few examples might be helpful:

1. In his book *A Token for Mourners: Or the Advice of Christ to a Distressed Mother, Bewailing the Death of Her Dear and Only Son* (1674),⁴² Flavel seeks to explain "where in the Boundaries of Sorrow are duly fixed, Excesses restrained, the common Pleas answered, and divers Rules for the support of God's afflicted Ones prescribed."⁴³ In other words, his primary aim is to help alleviate "bewailing," "distress," and "sorrow" caused by various external sufferings.

2. In *Preparation for Suffering, Or the Best Work in the Worst Times* (1681), Flavel seeks not to help people be physically "safe" in a dangerous world, but to prepare them internally and spiritually for the internal sufferings and pain brought about by external sufferings and pain.⁴⁴

1:425. Or, elsewhere: "Oh! it is a sad case, when inward and outward troubles meet together." *Preparation for Sufferings*, 6:75.

40. Flavel, *The Method of Grace*, 2:247.

41. Flavel, *Token for Mourners*, 5:609. Flavel writes, "Grief is a moth, which, getting into the mind, will, in a short time, make the body, be it never so strong and well-wrought a piece, like an old seary garment." *Token for Mourners*, 5:619.

42. First published as *A Token for Mourners: Or, the Advice of Christ to a Distressed Mother, Bewailing the Death of Her Dear and Only Son; Wherein the Boundaries of Sorrow Are Duly Fixed, Excesses Restrained, the Common Pleas Answered, and Divers Rules for the Support of Gods Afflicted Ones Prescribed*. (London: Turks-head in Cornhill, over against the Royal Exchange, 1674). It is interesting that Flavel accuses humanity of causing "excessive sorrows" by idolizing the temporal and fleeting things of this world, including other human beings (i.e., "loved ones"). *Balm of the Covenant*, 6:84.

43. Flavel, *Token for Mourners*, 5:604.

44. First published as *Preparation for Sufferings: Or, the Best Work in the Worst Times; Wherein the Necessity, Excellency, and Means of Our Readiness*

3. In *The Balm of the Covenant Applied to the Bleeding Wounds of Afflicted Saints* (c. 1688),[45] Flavel is not concerned about actual, physical bleeding wounds, but heart-wounds, or what Flavel calls "heavy burdens" of sorrow, disappointment, and internal discomfort. In particular, this is "the pain we feel at [a loved one's] parting."[46]

It is clear from these and other works that Flavel believed internal sufferings were more painful than external sufferings and, furthermore, that they could be alleviated by spiritual preparation.

Spiritual Suffering and the Effect of Satanic Activity

Flavel contends that spiritual suffering is of a different degree and category than the typical external and internal sufferings men and women experience in this world. He writes,

> Thou hast more reason to lament thy dead heart, than thy dead friend.... To lose the heavenly warmth and spiritual liveliness of thy affections, is undoubtedly a far more considerable loss, than to lose the wife of thy bosom, or the sweetest child that ever a tender parent laid in the grave.[47]

Flavel understood spiritual oppression and a deadness of faith to be foundational to the experience of internal suffering. That is why so much of his writing targets the spiritual health of his reader. Since

---

for Sufferings Are Evinced and Prescribed; Our Call to Suffering Cleared, and the Great Unreadiness of Many Profesours Bewailed. (London: Printed for Robert Boulter at the Turks-head in Cornhil, 1681).

45. The first edition's publication date is unknown. The second edition is *The Balm of the Covenant Applied to the Bleeding Wounds of Afflicted Saints: First Composed for the Relief of a Pious and Worthy Family, Mourning over the Deaths of Their Hopeful Children; And Now Made Publick for the Support of All Christians, Sorrowing on the Same or Any Other Account. To Which Is Added, a Sermon Preached for the Funeral of That Excellent and Religious Gentleman John Upton of Lupton* (London: Printed for J. Harris, at the Harrow against the Church in the Poultrey, 1688).

46. Flavel, *Balm of the Covenant*, 6:84.

47. Flavel, *Token for Mourners*, 5:619.

spiritual suffering is tied directly to sin, Flavel writes, "The least sin is more formidable to you than the greatest affliction: doubtless you would rather chuse to bury all your children, than provoke and grieve your heavenly Father."[48] Similarly, "spiritual distresses" are those afflictions brought about when "sin lay heavy,"[49] referring to instances in which a person experiences sin that seems overwhelming and hopeless. These spiritual sufferings and distresses are also closely connected to the onslaught of the evil forces raging against God and His elect. But how do the spiritual forces of evil and Satan relate to the spiritual suffering of humanity?

Flavel's understanding of Satan's involvement in the suffering of humanity is consistent with that of many of his Puritan contemporaries. Richard Sibbes, for example, taught that indwelling sin and Satan work together to cause suffering for an individual— physically, emotionally, and spiritually. Discouragements from these sufferings, he explains, "must come from ourselves and from Satan."[50] He continues: Our "disease of body [is] helped by Satan's malice."[51] Both physical suffering as well as internal grief brought on by indwelling sin "are helped forward by Satan" to the point of making "the life of many good Christians almost a martyrdom."[52] According to Sibbes, then, the reason why suffering exists at all is due to the sin of humanity, though it is "helped forward" by Satan. Similarly, Thomas Watson explains that some sufferings—like the breakdown of the family, suicide, and the effects of addiction—are the direct result of the temptation of Satan: "[Satan] tempts some to

---

48. Flavel, *Token for Mourners*, 5:626. Similarly, he writes, "Suffering is but a *respective, external,* and *temporal* evil; but sin is an universal, internal, and everlasting evil." *Preparation for Sufferings*, 6:63.
49. Flavel, *Token for Mourners*, 5:634.
50. Richard Sibbes, *The Bruised Reed* (London: Banner of Truth, 1998), 57. Originally published as *The Bruised Reed and Smoking Flax* (London: Printed for R. Dawlman, dwelling at the signe of the Brazen Serpent in Paul's Church-yard, 1630).
51. Sibbes, *Bruised Reed*, 57.
52. Sibbes, *Bruised Reed*, 47.

do away with themselves…and works some kind of inclination in the heart to embrace a temptation."[53]

Flavel's understanding of Satan's work is very similar to this and can be broken down in two distinct ways.[54] First, Flavel made a clear distinction between those who are under Satan's rule as Satan's children in this fallen world and those who are under God's rule as God's children in this fallen world. At birth, all humanity is under Satan's rule. Flavel writes, "Satan is the god of this world, all men by nature are his born subjects."[55] Moreover, Satan "possesses" both the body and soul of the unregenerate.[56] When God saves a person, He takes that person from the possession of Satan: "Christ never yet came into any soul in which Satan had not the possession before him. Every soul in which Christ dwells was once in Satan's power and possession."[57] Flavel reinforces the power of God in salvation against all of Satan's attempts to keep the soul from going to God. He writes, "Satan bids for the soul, Christ infinitely out-bids all his offers."[58] Though humans come naturally into this world under Satan's rule as an effect of original sin, Christ saves those who are His from Satan's dominion. However, as we shall see, that does not mean that Christ saves them from all future troubles and sufferings brought on by Satan.

The second method that Satan uses in bringing spiritual distress and suffering upon a person, according to Flavel, is that he continually tempts and entices humanity away from God. With this temptation, Satan attaches great affliction so as to breed even greater discontentment with God and His workings: "When it is dark night

---

53. Thomas Watson, *All Things for Good* (Edinburgh: Banner of Truth, 1986), 34. Watson, too, assumes Satan's work in causing sickness; see *All Things for Good*, 36.

54. Similarly, Flavel writes, "There is a twofold darkness, which gives Satan great advantage; the darkness of the *mind*, viz. ignorance; and the darkness of the *condition*, viz. trouble and affliction." *Token for Mourners*, 5:646.

55. Flavel, *England's Duty*, 4:204.
56. Flavel, *England's Duty*, 4:49.
57. Flavel, *England's Duty*, 4:213.
58. Flavel, *England's Duty*, 4:51.

with men, it is noon-day with Satan; i.e. our suffering-time is his busiest working-time; many a dismal suggestion he then plants, and grafts upon your affliction, which are much more dangerous to us than the affliction itself."[59]

The worship of anything else, according to Flavel, is idolatry. Therefore, Satan tempts people to worship even "good" things in the attempt to ultimately destroy them. According to Flavel, this is especially true of the believer. In his attempt to thwart God's redemptive purposes for the elect, Satan "bestirs himself to purpose" against the saints. Flavel writes, "O what showers of calumnies, and storms of persecution doth he pour upon the names and persons of Christ's faithful ambassadors!"[60] It is Satan who causes various sufferings, troubles, and trials—especially for God's people. It is upon the elect that "Satan...makes his sorest assaults and batteries."[61]

Flavel affirmed that one of Satan's key strategies is using humanity's indwelling sin and bringing that sin to actual fruition. Satan's "advantage," then, is to "assist our corruptions."[62] Flavel explains:

> [Satan] knows that which is already in motion is the more easily moved. In this confusion and hurry of thoughts he undiscernedly shuffles in his temptations. Sometimes aggravating the evils which we fear, with all the sinking and overwhelming circumstances imaginable; sometimes divining and fore-casting such events and evil, as (haply) never fall out. Sometimes repining at the disposes of God as more severe to us than to others; and sometimes reflecting, with very unbelieving and unworthy thoughts, upon the promises of God, and his faithfulness in them; by all which the affliction is made to sink deep into the soul before it actually comes. The thoughts are so disordered,

---

59. Flavel, *Token for Mourners*, 5:647. He adds, "Sometimes he injects *desponding* thoughts into the afflicted soul...sometimes murmuring and repining thoughts against the Lord.... And sometimes very *irreligious* and *atheistical* thoughts, as if there were no privilege to be had by religion." *Token for Mourners*, 5:647.
60. Flavel, *England's Duty*, 4:204.
61. Flavel, *Navigation Spiritualized*, 5:288.
62. Flavel, *Divine Conduct*, 4:491.

Flavel on the Origin and Nature of Suffering 27

that duty cannot be duly performed, and the soul is really weakened and disabled to bear its trial when it comes indeed.[63]

While our hearts are full of sin, deceitfulness, and inconsistency, "such [is] the malice, policy, and diligence of Satan to improve these."[64] Flavel's exhortation is that, when this happens and suffering is furthered by Satan's ploys, the Christian "resign his will to God's and quietly commit the events and issues of all to him, whatever they may prove."[65] This quiet committal, then, dovetails with Flavel's exhortation to respond to suffering with quiet submission.

It should especially be noted that, according to Flavel, the primary sufferings brought about by Satan are spiritual in nature. While Satan certainly has influence over physical suffering, he primarily attacks people spiritually. One of the greatest spiritual sufferings brought against believers, in particular, is internal discouragement, sorrow, and guilt over sin. Satan tempts believers to think that they have sinned so greatly and too many times, that they are beyond the acceptance, forgiveness, and love of God.[66] Satan also seeks to make the believer's delight in God not a joy, but a "terror." He tries to distract the believer's thoughts of God and of God's goodness, tempts the believer to become spiritually proud, and seeks to cut off any hope he or she may have. These, Flavel explains, are part of Satan's tactics in bringing spiritual suffering upon individuals.[67]

One of the interesting points about Flavel's understanding of Satan's design for suffering is that Satan brings about internal suffering by tempting people with external pleasures. In other words, external delights and comforts can actually turn to become the catalyst for internal and spiritual suffering. Flavel writes, "Satan bids riches, honours, and pleasures, with ease and quietness to the flesh in the enjoyment of them."[68] But all these things, Flavel argues, can lead to

---

63. Flavel, *Divine Conduct*, 4:491–92.
64. Flavel, *Antipharmacum Saluberrimum*, 4:553.
65. Flavel, *Divine Conduct*, 4:492.
66. Flavel, *England's Duty*, 4:138, 156.
67. Flavel, *Divine Conduct*, 4:473; Flavel, *England's Duty*, 4:182, 253.
68. Flavel, *England's Duty*, 4:93.

enslavement, entanglements, sorrow, despair, and ruin.[69] Elsewhere, Flavel writes, "O how many have been coached to hell in the chariots of earthly pleasures, while others have been whipped to heaven by the rod of affliction!"[70] In an attempt to escape the external sufferings of the world, Satan leads people into greater internal and spiritual sufferings.

Perhaps with greater irony, Flavel maintains that Satan tempts people away from Christ by causing them to realize the great external sufferings brought about by following Christ: "[Satan] bids [the soul] to look upon the train of troubles and afflictions that come along with Christ.... If Christ come in, reproaches, losses, and sufferings will certainly come in with him; troops of miseries and calamities follow him."[71] Therefore, the lure of earthly pleasures can actually lead to greater suffering. That is why Flavel devotes an entire work to how believers ought to use and enjoy earthly things and earthly work in *Husbandry Spiritualized: The Heavenly Use of Earthly Things* (1669). In addition, Satan tempts people to perform the outward duties of religion so that "true" religion and fellowship with God will fall by the wayside. Those who only attain a "partial reformation" will likewise often experience internal and spiritual distress and affliction.[72]

While Satan tempts and afflicts all people everywhere—whether by his ruling over them or indirectly—he will continue to afflict unbelievers in the world to come: "He that *tempts* now, will *torment* then."[73] Notwithstanding, in all these actions of Satan, he is never removed from God's ultimate and sovereign control. Flavel writes that God has "ordered the very malice of Satan, and the wickedness of men, as an occasion of eternal good to [the elect's] souls."[74] Even in the way in which Satan uses humanity's indwelling sin to further it for greater evil, God ultimately allows him "to mingle his temptations and injects

---

69. Flavel, *England's Duty*, 4:93.
70. Flavel, *A Saint Indeed*, 5:438.
71. Flavel, *England's Duty*, 4:102.
72. Flavel, *England's Duty*, 4:101.
73. Flavel, *England's Duty*, 4:49.
74. Flavel, *Divine Conduct*, 4:382.

with [our sin]."⁷⁵ At no point, then, does Satan rule on his own apart from the overruling sovereign hand of God; and this for God's own glory and the ultimate good of His people. Flavel sees all sufferings—physical, internal, and spiritual—as ultimately good for those who love God and are called according to His purpose.⁷⁶ He explains:

> Although the people of God meet with many seeming rubs and set-backs in their way to heaven, which are like contrary winds to a ship; yet they are from the day of their conversion to the day of their complete salvation, never out of a trade-wind's way to heaven. Rom. viii. 21. [sic]. "We know that all things work together for good to them that love God, to them that are called according to his purpose." This is a most precious scripture, pregnant with its consolation, to all believers in all conditions, a pillar of comfort to all distressed saints.⁷⁷

The internal "distress" that Flavel writes of is bound together with the spiritual life of the individual. This is evident in the way Flavel counsels, instructs, and comforts the believer.

Peter Lewis, in *The Genius of Puritanism*, writes, "The Puritan pastor exercised his pastoral functions in four ways, *viz.*—catechizing, counseling, comforting and sharing with his people times of special private worship."⁷⁸ Lewis contends that spiritual sufferings, like spiritual depressions, "were most usually caused by a lack of the sense of God's presence with the believer in love, grace and power."⁷⁹ This kind of pastoral role, as we have seen, is certainly true of Flavel's approach. Flavel sought to encourage his reader to have a stronger faith in the God who ordains all things for the good of His people. Indeed, all "afflictions, temptations, corruption, desertions,

---

75. Flavel, *England's Duty*, 4:229.
76. Cf. Rom. 8:28.
77. Flavel, *Navigation Spiritualized*, 5:279. The biblical quote actually comes from Romans 8:28.
78. Peter Lewis, *The Genius of Puritanism* (Morgan, Pa.: Soli Deo Gloria, 1996), 63.
79. Lewis, *Genius of Puritanism*, 66.

&c." help the believer "onward" to heaven.[80] By "desertions," Flavel speaks of what we might term "depression" today. As Lewis explains, desertion was "a particular and radical form of spiritual depression."[81] These internal distresses are closely bound up with the individual's sin—in not having the eyes of faith to see how all things work together for their good. One of Flavel's poems in *Navigation Spiritualized* summarizes his understanding on this point:

> All their afflictions, rightly understood,
> Are blessings; ev'ry wind will blow some good
> Sure at their troubles saints would never grudge,
> Were sense deposed, and faith made the judge.
> Falls make them warier, amend their pace;
> When gift puff up their hearts, and weaken grace.
> Could Satan see the issue, and th' event
> Of his temptations, he would scarcely tempt.
> Could saints but see what fruits their troubles bring,
> Amidst those troubles they would shout and sing.
> O sacred wisdom! who can but admire
> To see how thou dost save from fire, by fire!
> No doubt but saints in glory wond'ring stand
> At those strange methods few now understand.[82]

Flavel understands afflictions to be actual blessings for the elect, used in the sanctification of the saints, whether they be external, internal, or spiritual. All suffering—though stemming from Adam's fall in the garden—is ultimately decreed from all eternity and brought forth into time and space by God's providential ordering. It is to this doctrine of God's sovereignty that we now turn.

---

80. Flavel, *Navigation Spiritualized*, 5:280.
81. Lewis, *Genius of Puritanism*, 66. Lewis explains that desertions "did not mean that God had truly deserted the elect soul, but the term describes the experience man-ward and as it appeared to the subject, in which the 'lively' sense of God's presence and a favourable share or 'interest' in it was denied to the Christian." Thus, spiritual depression and desertion became "synonymous in Puritan parlance."
82. Flavel, *Navigation Spiritualized*, 5:281.

CHAPTER THREE

Flavel on Divine Sovereignty and Human Suffering

Alexandra Walsham, professor of modern history at the University of Cambridge, argues that the doctrine of God's providence was not an isolated belief among the Puritans, but rather a mainline belief in seventeenth-century England—only differentiated by varying degrees rather than by substance. She writes, "Providentialism was not a marginal feature of the religious culture of early modern England, but part of the mainstream, a cluster of presuppositions which enjoyed near universal acceptance."[1] John Spurr, in his book *English Puritanism, 1603–1689*, concurs: "[The] Puritans took their belief in divine providence, the guiding hand of God in all earthly affairs, to greater lengths than their protestant neighbors."[2] In other words, what made the Puritans' element stand out with relation to God's sovereignty and providence was their emphasis upon God's sovereignty and their desire to attain full assurance that they were indeed members of God's elect.

The Doctrine of God's Sovereignty in Seventeenth-Century Puritanism

What was *providence*, as understood by the English Puritans? According to Walsham, providence "was a learned technical term for an elaborate theological doctrine which they used as an evocative

---

1. Alexandra Walsham, *Providence in Early Modern England* (Oxford: Oxford University Press, 1999), 2.
2. Spurr, *English Puritanism*, 183.

shorthand for the powerful spiritual presence they detected within and around them."[3] Likewise, Francis Bremer has observed, "Puritans believed that the final outcome of the life of individuals and of mankind was preordained, and referred to the divine blueprint for human history as providence."[4] The theology of God's sovereignty and its theological counterpart—providence—as it continued to be developed by the Puritan element in England through preaching and writing, played a key role in forging a Protestant consciousness and confessional identity that stood directly opposed to the "popery" of England's past.[5]

John Flavel's *Divine Conduct*

John Flavel's *Divine Conduct; Or, the Mystery of Providence* (1678) is arguably the most extensive work on the sovereignty of God by a seventeenth-century English Puritan.[6] Joel R. Beeke calls it the best Puritan work on divine providence.[7] Sinclair Ferguson writes that of all Flavel's works, "none speaks with more power" than this "spiritual classic."[8] Many Christians over the centuries have noted their particular indebtedness to *Divine Conduct*. Mark Deckard points

---

3. Walsham, *Providence in Early Modern England*, 2.

4. Francis J. Bremer, *Puritanism: A Very Short Introduction* (Oxford: Oxford University Press, 2009), 45.

5. Walsham, *Providence in Early Modern England*, 5.

6. Originally published as *Divine Conduct; Or, the Mysterie of Providence. Wherein the Being and Efficacy of Providence Is Asserted and Vindicated; The Methods of Providence As It Passes through the Several Stages of Our Lives Opened; And the Proper Course of Improving All Providences Directed, in a Treatise upon Psalm 57. Ver. 2* (London: Printed by R. W. for Francis Tyton at the Three Daggers in Fleetstreet, 1678).

7. Joel R. Beeke, *A Reader's Guide to Reformed Literature: An Annotated Bibliography of Reformed Theology* (Grand Rapids: Reformation Heritage Books, 1999), 27–28. Beeke also notes that the "second-best" is Stephen Charnock's "A Treatise on Divine Providence," in *Complete Works* (Edinburgh: James Nichol, 1864), 1:3–120.

8. Sinclair B. Ferguson, "Divine Conduct by John Flavel (1628–1691)," in *The Devoted Life: An Invitation to the Puritan Classics*, ed. Kelly M. Kapic and Randall C. Gleason (Downers Grove, Ill.: IVP, 2004), 211.

out that it is as practical in our present day as it was in Flavel's.[9] Michael Boland, in his "Publisher's Introduction" to the stand-alone Banner of Truth edition, writes, "To learn of the Providence of God under the tuition of John Flavel will bring Christian believers into a sphere they never reckoned with before."[10]

There is little doubt that *Divine Conduct* is Flavel's best-known work, seen not only by its use in a wide variety of secondary sources but also through its continual reprints by The Banner of Truth Trust.[11] For this reason, and because it articulates Flavel's doctrine of divine sovereignty as a whole, it will be the primary text for this chapter's discussion.

Divine Conduct centers on Psalm 57:2: "I will cry unto God most high; unto God that performeth all things for me."[12] Because God's ways and thoughts are higher than human ways and thoughts, God's work of providence is mysterious. Although there is nothing in Scripture or in the works of God that is repugnant to sound reason, Flavel contends that "there are some things in both, which are opposite to carnal reason…and therefore our reason never shews itself more unreasonable, than in summoning those things to its bar, which transcends its sphere and capacity."[13] In other words, Flavel warns his reader not to carry an unworthy suspicion or skepticism about God's providence simply because he or she does not understand the things that take place.

One of these great "mysteries" lies in the area of suffering and why God not only allows it but ordains it.[14] It should be noted that the "mystery" of God's providence lies not in the fact that God ordains

---

9. Mark Deckard, *Helpful Truth in Past Places: The Puritan Practice of Biblical Counseling* (Ross-Shire, Scotland: Christian Focus, 2009), 18–21.

10. Michael Boland, publisher's introduction to *Divine Conduct*, by John Flavel (Edinburgh: Banner of Truth, 2009), 14.

11. Since 1963, The Banner of Truth Trust has issued nine reprints, the most recent being in 2009.

12. Quoted in Flavel, *Divine Conduct*, 4:342.

13. Flavel, *Divine Conduct*, 4:435.

14. Chapter 4 will address this topic in depth.

suffering but rather *why* He ordains suffering at specific times and in specific places. While we know some of the reasons God ordains suffering generally—which will be examined later—we may not know the exact reason when it comes. This, Flavel argues, is mysterious. For this reason, Flavel devotes much of the work to explaining that end. Whether good or harm comes upon us, we cannot ultimately know God's thoughts or purposes. Flavel writes: "We cannot understand the mind and heart of God, by the things he dispenseth with his hand. If prosperous providences befal us, we cannot say, Herein is a sure sign that God loves me.... And from these adverse, afflictive providences we cannot know his hatred.... Yet the *manner* in which they befal us, and the effects and fruits they produce in us, do distinguish them very manifestly; and by them we may discern whether they be sanctified providences, and the fruits of the love of God, or not."[15]

Divine Conduct is divided into eight sections, each exhorting the reader to meditate upon and apply the doctrine of divine providence. In his opening address to the reader, Flavel states his purpose: "The pleasantest history that ever we read in our lives.... The ensuing treatise is an essay to that purpose, in which thou wilt find some remarks set upon Providence in its passage through the several stages of our lives." He adds, "My hearty prayer is that providence will direct this treatise to such hands in such seasons, and so bless and prosper its design, that God may have glory, thou mayest have benefit, and myself comfort in the success thereof, who am, Thine and the church's servant, In the hand of Providence, John Flavel."[16]

Interestingly, his purpose in *Divine Conduct* parallels his understanding of the overall purpose of providence, which Flavel sees as "steering all to the port of [God's] own praise and his people's happiness."[17] God's glory and the elect's joy, then, are Flavel's twin goals as he unpacks the doctrine of divine sovereignty.

---

15. Flavel, *Divine Conduct*, 4:479–80.
16. Flavel, *Divine Conduct*, 4:341–42.
17. Flavel, *Divine Conduct*, 4:340.

Flavel's Doctrine of the Sovereignty of God

At the outset, it is appropriate to note what Flavel means by *sovereignty* and how he relates it to God's decree and providence. This is also important as we build his theology of how God is sovereign over suffering. Flavel writes, "[God's] *sovereignty* is gloriously displayed in his *eternal decrees*, and *temporal providences*."[18] Professor Walsham argues that the seventeenth-century Puritan element as a whole held to this "dual definition" that comprised both God's decree—which necessarily assumes infinite knowledge—and the execution of that decree by God's power. Furthermore, there was not an area or object over which God did not exert absolute sovereignty. She notes, "God's sovereignty extended from the most contemptible of His creatures to the celestial, from the basest creeping worm, tiniest gnat, and fly to the noblest angels in heaven."[19] Flavel, then, finds agreement with his Puritan contemporaries.

Humanity can have knowledge of God's sovereignty by comprehending—despite the limitations of the finite mind—these two elements of God's eternal decree and temporal providence. In other words, decree and providence are the two ways in which sovereignty is "displayed" and manifested. This is a crucial element in Flavel's theology: when Flavel speaks of providence, he assumes a theological assumption of divine sovereignty. As we shall see, Flavel maintains a close relationship between a theology of sovereignty and its practical application. That is why he stresses the term *providence* throughout—not because he doesn't see the need to stress sovereignty, but because providence is the practical outworking of sovereignty.

God's sovereignty, according to Flavel, must be interpreted through the lens of God's special revelation, the Bible, which sets out God's sovereignty in His written decrees and laws. Flavel explains, "For the absolute sovereignty of God, which is his glory,

---

18. Flavel, *Divine Conduct*, 4:426. Elsewhere, he writes, "The glorious sovereignty of God is illustriously displayed in two things, his decrees and his providences." *Token for Mourners*, 5:627.

19. Walsham, *Providence in Early Modern England*, 9.

1 Tim. vi. 15. is manifested in two things especially; in his decrees, Rom. ix. 20. and in his laws, Isa. xxxiii. 22."[20] Perhaps more clearly, Flavel writes, "In all your observation of providence have special respect to that word of God which is fulfilled and made good to you thereby. This is a clear truth, that all providences have relation to the written word."[21] What does he mean by a "relation" to the written Word? Flavel sees that where Scripture speaks of warnings, counsel, or promises (to name a few), he sees them fulfilled by God's sovereignty in action; namely, God's providence. "Providence," Flavel writes, "[works] in concurrence with the word" and "no testimony of providence is to be accepted against the word."[22]

Flavel argues that the believer should investigate and meditate upon God's Word in relation to the course of events in history so that the truth of God's providence is confirmed in the believer's mind and heart. In other words, Flavel sees God's sovereignty manifested in the events of history. In addition, he argues that when a believer makes note of God's providential acts faithfully, he or she will be instructed as to his or her duties to God. Flavel summarizes this close relationship between Scripture and providence: "The word interprets the works of God. Providences in themselves are not a perfect guide.... Well then, bring those providences you have past through, or are now under, to the word; and you will find yourselves surrounded with a marvelous light; and see the verification of the scriptures in them."[23] Therefore, God's providences must be interpreted through the lens of the Bible so that the Christian may be wise in understanding and live in right obedience to God. Scripture is God's revealed will, meant to inform humanity of aspects of His secret will. Hence, Flavel separates God's will into His secret and revealed will. The latter is manifested in the Bible and in works of creation—the will that is effective and what Flavel understands to be God's providence. His secret will, or

---

20. Flavel, *Antipharmacum Saluberrimum*, 4:523.
21. Flavel, *Divine Conduct*, 4:419.
22. Flavel, *Divine Conduct*, 4:470.
23. Flavel, *Divine Conduct*, 4:419.

"commanding will," is synonymous with what Flavel understands as God's eternal "decree."[24] The believer's task is to submit to the will of God in a "prudent and diligent" way by looking to what Flavel calls the true "compass"—the Word of God—which navigates "us in our course to heaven."[25]

What does Flavel mean when he speaks of God's sovereignty? When he uses this terminology, what is he saying about God's character? First, Flavel believes that sovereignty is an attribute that is "incommunicable," which means that God does not share this characteristic with any other being in the universe.[26] He also maintains that God alone is "infinitely superior...so that we and all we have proceed from his will."[27] In addition, he links God's "absolute will" with God's "indisputable sovereignty," thereby suggesting that it is an attribute that cannot diminish or wane in any way.[28] God's sovereignty, therefore, is directly related to His power, authority, and will.

Flavel asks the reader, "WHAT is the power of God?" Answer: "An essential property of his nature, whereby he can do all things that he pleases to have done."[29] The only things that God cannot do are those things that are inconsistent with His truth and character (e.g., denying himself). God's power "hath no bounds nor limits but the pleasure and will of God." Thus, "divine pleasure is the only rule according to which Divine Power exerts itself in the world."[30] To summarize, then, Flavel writes, "The power of God is a supreme and sovereign power, from which all creature-power is derived, and by which it is over-ruled, restrained, and limited at his pleasure."[31]

Flavel also argues that God has the right to order and grant permission to His creatures as He so desires. Even though man is

---

24. Flavel, *Divine Conduct*, 4:468.
25. Flavel, *Navigation Spiritualized*, 5:256, 268.
26. Flavel, *Antipharmacum Saluberrimum*, 4:523.
27. Flavel, *Divine Conduct*, 4:426.
28. Flavel, *Navigation Spiritualized*, 5:231–32.
29. Flavel, *Exposition of the Assembly's Catechism*, 6:151.
30. Flavel, *The Righteous Man's Refuge*, 3:345.
31. Flavel, *Righteous Man's Refuge*, 3:345.

unable to obey apart from God's sovereign grace, "God hath not lost his right to command."[32] Flavel blends sovereignty with authority in the source of God's right to give commands: "These be commands flowing from sovereignty, clothed with the highest authority."[33] To be sure, however, only the elect have the ability to obey these commands. He writes, "The duty indeed is ours, but the power by which alone we perform it is God's: we act as we are acted by the Spirit."[34] Providence, in Flavel's thought, has a particular eye on the people of God, so that providence toward the saints becomes "the performance of God's gracious purposes and promises to his people."[35] Moreover, when God is said to "permit" something, it should be understood as the other side of God "commanding" something—these are two sides of the same coin. Many times, Flavel combines them. For example, he writes of suffering that comes upon the ministers of the Word: "God hath permitted and ordered some weaning providence to befall" them.[36] However, Flavel argues that the believer should learn certain principles along with each providence: "There is truly a principle of quietness in the permitting, as in the commanding will of God.... For it is inconsistent with the wisdom of a common agent to permit any thing, which he might prevent if he pleased, to cross his great design and end."[37] Thus Flavel holds these two elements together as two ways of thinking about God's sovereignty displayed.

Against Deism: Flavel's Understanding of "Secondary Causes"

In chapter 1, we noted that Flavel's theology fell in line with Calvin and Owen, contra Kwai Sing Chang's assertion that Flavel stood somewhere between Owen and Baxter.[38] Calvin writes that, while the Christian should believe that "nothing takes place by chance"

---

32. Flavel, *England's Duty*, 4:190.
33. Flavel, *Antipharmacum Saluberrimum*, 4:519.
34. Flavel, *Divine Conduct*, 4:490.
35. Flavel, *Divine Conduct*, 4:345.
36. Flavel, *A Treatise of the Soul of Man*, 2:600.
37. Flavel, *A Saint Indeed*, 5:447.
38. Chang, "John Flavel of Dartmouth," 69.

and that God is the "principal cause of things," he or she "will give attention to the secondary causes in their proper place."[39] Similarly, he says, "a godly man will not overlook the secondary causes."[40] Alexandra Walsham has observed that the Puritans did not understand their Creator as a watchmaker deity who set the order of the world in motion only to kick back and watch it all play out.[41] Rather, as Richard Sibbes points out, for example, "God doth not put things into a frame, and then leave them to their own motion, as we do clocks, after we have set them right."[42] In like manner, Thomas Watson writes, "Care, when it is *excentrick,* either distrustfull, or distracting, is very dishonorable to God; it takes away his providence, as if he sate in heaven, and minded not what became of things here below; like a man that makes a clock, and then leaves it to go off it self."[43]

The world, according to the Puritans, "was not a machine that ran automatically according to an initial plan."[44] Rather, God created the world and subsequently orders and governs His creation by His providence. These questions, then, are before us: Did Flavel follow Calvin and find agreement with his Puritan contemporaries on the doctrine of sovereignty? Furthermore, did he hold to a similar position of first and secondary causes and a belief that ran counter to deistic thought?

In *The Art of Suffering and the Impact of Seventeenth-Century Anti-Providential Thought*, Ann Thompson seems to suggest that Flavel employed the use of the deistic understanding of a "clockwork universe" with reference to God's sovereignty. Is this proposition true?

---

39. John Calvin, *Institutes of the Christian Religion*, ed. John T. McNeill, trans. Ford Lewis Battles (Philadelphia: Westminster Press, 1960), 1.17.6.

40. Calvin, *Institutes*, 1.17.9.

41. Walsham, *Providence in Early Modern England*, 10.

42. Richard Sibbes, *The Soul's Conflict with Itself,* in *The Complete Works of Richard Sibbes*, ed. Alexander Balloch Grosart (Edinburgh: James Nichol, 1862), 1:204.

43. Thomas Watson, *The Art of Divine Contentment* (London: Printed by T. M. for Ralph Smith, at the sign of the Bible in Cornhil, neer the Royal Exchange, 1654), 3.

44. Bremer and Webster, eds., *Puritans and Puritanism*, 45.

Did Flavel believe that God had set the course of creation in motion and then left it alone? Contrary to Thompson, it shall be made clear that Flavel did not hold to a deistic understanding of God's control, creation, or the use of "secondary causes."[45]

Thompson bases her argument on Flavel's use of the phrase "natural causes," quoting from *Divine Conduct*, in which Flavel speaks of how God delivers His people "against the course of natural causes" and that there exists a "suspension" in these causes by God's sovereign hand.[46] While Flavel certainly uses these terms, as mentioned in chapter 1, Thompson misreads Flavel's theology of the use of secondary causes. Indeed, in the very next paragraphs and pages of *Divine Conduct* (from which Thompson quotes Flavel's view of natural causes), Flavel explains that God governs even the intimate details of these "natural causes" to His own ends.[47] The day-to-day events, storms, and actions of people cannot be "wholly swayed by the course of nature."[48] While "reason lays [these events] according to the rules of nature; providence crosses its hands…and orders quite contrary issues and events."[49]

Walsham points out, "Most divines insisted that God…was not 'so tied to second causes, as when they faile, his Providence ceaseth unto us.'"[50] As we shall see, Flavel does not regard "natural causes" or "secondary causes" relating to a course of nature as being separated from God's immediate and providential governing. He remarks, "Who can but see the finger of God in these things!"[51]

---

45. Flavel does mention the illustration of the clock, but only with relation to understanding small parts of theology as they relate to the greater body of Christian doctrine, not God's sovereignty or providence. *Fountain of Life*, 1:21. At no point does Flavel use the idea of God putting the course of events in motion, as in winding up a clock, and then watching them all play out.
46. Thompson, *Art of Suffering*, 9. Cf. Flavel, *Divine Conduct*, 4:351.
47. Flavel, *Divine Conduct*, 4:353.
48. Flavel, *Divine Conduct*, 4:354.
49. Flavel, *Divine Conduct*, 4:354.
50. Walsham, *Providence in Early Modern England*, 12, quoting Ralph Walker, *A Learned and Profitable Treatise of God's Providence* (1608).
51. Flavel, *Divine Conduct*, 4:356.

While Flavel certainly recognizes a general "common rule of second causes," God's power and providence overshadow these, and they work as His will directs, immediately according to His sovereign pleasure.[52] All "secondary causes"—people, weather, social events, and so forth—necessarily depend on God for their ability and are under the permission of His supreme power.[53] In explaining these "second causes" with relation to God's providence, Flavel writes negatively against the sinful patterns of humanity: "Do we not, my brethren, look upon second causes as if they had the main stroke in our business? And with a neglective eye pass by God, as if he came in but collaterally, and on the bye, into it? But certainly all endeavours will be unsanctified, if not successless in which God is not eyed and engaged."[54] Even though it may seem that a person is comforted and delivered by natural or secondary causes, it is ultimately and fully God's providential working. As Flavel summarizes: "All secondary means of deliverance and comfort necessarily depend upon the will and pleasure of God, and signify nothing without him."[55]

Moreover, Flavel maintains a constant eye on humanity's responsibility and duty, therefore denying the opposite extreme of determinism or fatalism: "Walk therefore suitably to this obligation of Providence."[56] Again, "If God plant, and fence, and water you by providence, sure he looks you should bring forth fruit.... Be active for that God, who is acting every moment for you."[57] Even when it comes to God's sovereign choice in election, Flavel argues, "The only way to make [election] sure is by striving and giving all diligence in the way of duty."[58]

---

52. Flavel, *Righteous Man's Refuge*, 3:345.
53. Flavel, *Exposition of the Assembly's Catechism*, 6:152.
54. Flavel, *Navigation Spiritualized*, 5:267–68. Thus when Flavel uses terms such as "second causes" or even "laws of nature" (cf. *Balm of the Covenant*, 6:84), he does not divorce these from God's immediate and immanent providence and governance.
55. Flavel, *Seaman's Companion*, 5:356.
56. Flavel, *Divine Conduct*, 4:401, 419–21.
57. Flavel, *Divine Conduct*, 4:465.
58. Flavel, *Caution to Seamen*, 5:339.

One of the clearest passages Flavel writes against a deistic view of providence is his explanation that "the Divine providence is not more signally discovered in governing the motions of the clouds, than it is in disposing and ordering the spirits and motions of the ministers of the gospel." As every cloud cannot move along but by the providential governing of God, so "neither can gospel-ministers chuse their own stations, and govern their own motions, but must go when and where the Spirit and providence of God directs and guides them."[59] Furthermore, Flavel explains, "[God] commandeth and raiseth the stormy winds. This is God's prerogative: none can raise winds but himself." While there is indeed a "natural cause of winds," it "doth not at all restrain the absolute sovereignty of God over them."[60]

When Flavel writes of "natural causes" or "laws" of things, he understands these terms as they seem to the senses of humanity—like the seemingly arbitrary blowing of winds or the flight of a bird. In reality, however, "all its motions are ordered of the Lord."[61] The idea that God has set these things in motion and then simply watches as they unfold is certainly not Flavel's understanding of God's sovereignty or of the events of this world. According to Flavel, God is immanent, active, and involved in every movement of a cloud, every flight of a bird, and every "motion" of humanity.

In opposition to Chang (who argues that Flavel had leanings toward Baxterianism) and Thompson (who suggests that Flavel had leanings toward deism), then, Flavel's understanding of sovereignty is immensely relational, actual, and portrayed in harmony with God's imminence and omnipresence—which is why he stresses providence as the personal outworking of sovereignty in everyday life. While Flavel supports God's "absolute sovereignty,"[62] he does not venture into a deistic, impersonal theology of God's control over history.

---

59. Flavel, *Preparation for Sufferings*, 6:4.
60. Flavel, *Seaman's Companion*, 5:360.
61. Flavel, *Seaman's' Companion*, 5:360.
62. Flavel, *Antipharmacum Saluberrimum*, 4:523.

God's Sovereignty Displayed in Eternal Decree

Flavel believed that everything that happens in history is part of God's eternal plan; whatever comes to pass takes place because of God's decretal will. As we shall see, this includes suffering. Following the Westminster Shorter Catechism, Flavel writes, "The decrees of God are his eternal purpose, according to the council of his will, whereby for his own glory he hath fore-ordained whatsoever comes to pass."[63] Flavel believed that nothing happens outside or apart from God's decrees, "even the smallest [of things]."[64]

God's decrees extend from His infinite wisdom and are not conditional in any way upon the actions and choices of His creation. Rather, "the decrees of God are most free, all flowing from the mere pleasure of his will."[65] God's decretal will stands for eternity and is executed by immanent providence in the actual course of time. Of God's grace in salvation coming as the blend of eternal decree and temporal providence, Flavel writes, "Providence had a design upon you for your eternal good, which you understood not: the time of mercy was now fully come; the decree was now ready to bring forth that mercy with which it had gone big from eternity, and its gracious design must be executed by the hand of providence."[66] This is consistent with Flavel's theology of election and predestination, for the justifying act in salvation, "which God from all eternity, purely out of his benevolent love, purpose and decreed for his elect, was also in time purchased for them by the death of Christ."[67]

Because God is omniscient, omnipotent, and eternal, God's decrees do not change; they, like Him, are immutable and eternal.[68] Therefore, nothing happens by chance, but rather they happen

---

63. Flavel, *Exposition of the Assembly's Catechism*, 6:160.
64. Flavel, *Exposition of the Assembly's Catechism*, 6:160.
65. Flavel, *Exposition of the Assembly's Catechism*, 6:161.
66. Flavel, *Divine Conduct*, 4:385–86.
67. Flavel, *A Brief Account of the Rise and Growth of Antinomianism, with Reflections upon the Errors of the Sect*, 3:559.
68. Flavel, *Divine Conduct*, 4:466.

through His decrees, executed in time "in the works of creation and providence."[69] Flavel exhorts his reader, "We ought to ascribe nothing to chance, but to the appointment or providence of God."[70] The decrees of God and the promises of God are the two sides of the sovereignty coin. Flavel explains, "Promises, like a pregnant woman, must accomplish their appointed months, and when they have so done, providence will midwife the mercies they go big withal into the world, and not one of them shall miscarry."[71] Promises, then, are revealed decrees—both extending from God's sovereignty: "Providence [is] the execution of God's decree, and the fulfilling of his word."[72] To this subject of providence, then, we now turn.

God's Sovereignty Displayed in Providence

Providence, according to Flavel, is the fulfillment and execution of God's eternal decree. Both providence and decree, as we have seen, are expressions of God's sovereignty and are the ways in which sovereignty is "displayed." What are God's "works" of providence? Concurring with the Westminster Shorter Catechism, Flavel argues, "God's works of providence are his most holy, wise, and powerful preserving and governing all his creatures, and all their actions."[73] It should be noted, once again, that Flavel continually points his reader to the Scriptures as the authoritative foundation upon which he builds his case. His assumption is that the reader acknowledges this authority and therefore should not only plainly see that the Bible teaches the doctrine of divine providence, but also that the reader should therefore be convinced of this teaching by reasonable faith.[74] Scripture and the Spirit of God work in conjunction with

---

69. Flavel, *Exposition of the Assembly's Catechism*, 6:162.
70. Flavel, *Exposition of the Assembly's Catechism*, 6:161.
71. Flavel, *Divine Conduct*, 4:472.
72. Flavel, *Divine Conduct*, 4:346.
73. Flavel, *Exposition of the Assembly's Catechism*, 6:164.
74. Indeed, most of Flavel's question-and-answer format in his *Exposition of the Assembly's Shorter Catechism* is replete with biblical notation and references. At times, his answers to his series of questions are little more than

divine providence. He writes, "The most wise God orders the dispensations of providence in a blessed subordination to the work of his Spirit. There is a sweet harmony betwixt them in their distinct workings. They all meet in that one blessed issue which God hath, by the counsel of his will, directed them to.... Hence it is, that the Spirit is said to be in, and to order the motions of the wheels of providence, Ezek. i. 20. and so they move together by consent."[75] Thus the Word and Spirit work with, in, and through God's eternal decrees brought forth in temporal providences.

In this "preserving" and "governing," God upholds all things by the word of His power so that, by Him, all things consist.[76] That God preserves all His creatures and all their actions means, according to Flavel, that God sustains and provides for them. This includes elements of God's common grace to all of humanity—food, rain, sunshine, and shelter. The only reason that both "man and beast" are able to survive and have any enjoyment in this life is solely because God sustains, provides, and preserves them.[77]

The second act of providence is that God governs all His creatures and all their actions. Both God's preserving and His governing are "common and general over all," but "special and peculiar to some men."[78] In other words, Flavel's theology of providence entails sovereign preservation and governance over all of humanity, but with a special eye toward God's elect—evidenced in the promise that all things work together for good for those who love God and are called according to His purpose.[79] But all of the actions of God's creatures happen by the preserving and governing of God.

---

direct quotations from the Bible. See *Exposition of the Assembly's Catechism*, 6:164–66. Flavel argues that providence can be plainly seen in "scripture testimonies," "scripture emblems," and the sure accomplishment of "scripture predictions"—all of which provide "evidence" of divine providence.

75. Flavel, *Divine Conduct*, 4:406.
76. Cf. Hebrews 1:3 and Colossians 1:17.
77. Flavel, *Exposition of the Assembly's Catechism*, 6:165.
78. Flavel, *Exposition of the Assembly's Catechism*, 6:165.
79. Cf. Romans 8:28.

Flavel argues that the providence of God is "holy," which means that it is morally righteous. It is also "wise" and "powerful." God does whatsoever He desires to do and nothing can thwart or "stay his hand."[80] What are the practical implications of this? First, "God's people are safe amidst all their enemies and dangers"; second, "prayer is the best expedient to prosperity and success of lawful affairs" because God is near to them who call upon Him; third, "God's people should rest quietly in the care of his providence for them in all their straits"; and, fourth, "it is no small privilege to be adopted children of God, and the members of Christ; for all is ordered for their eternal good."[81] In other words, the Christian should find great comfort and peace from the doctrine of divine providence because God has his or her eternal good in sight—despite the suffering and "straits" he or she endures in this lifetime.

Flavel labors to set forth this practical instruction of providence for the elect, which he argues "is nothing else but the performance of God's gracious purposes and promises to his people.... Grace makes the promise, and providence the payment."[82] God has a specific and particular "interest and influence" in all things concerning the elect "throughout their lives, from first to last." Even the "most minute and ordinary affairs" of the believer's life are "transacted and managed by [providence]."[83] Furthermore, God's providential actions are irresistible. They effectually accomplish His purpose and design. Even when the Christian starts to think that all things are against him or her, "providence neither doth, nor can do any thing that is really against the true interest and good of the saints" so that "there is nothing but good to the saints in God's purposes and promises."[84] Flavel, therefore, sees divine providence as a supporting and encouraging doctrine for the believer, especially in times of suffering. He adds this doctrinal conclusion: "It is the duty

---

80. Flavel, *Exposition of the Assembly's Catechism*, 6:165.
81. Flavel, *Exposition of the Assembly's Catechism*, 6:165–66.
82. Flavel, *Divine Conduct*, 4:345.
83. Flavel, *Divine Conduct*, 4:346.
84. Flavel, *Divine Conduct*, 4:346.

of the saints, especially in times of straits, to reflect upon the performances of providence for them in all the states, and through all the stages of their lives."[85]

Flavel's theology of sovereignty sees God's righteous and wise omnipotence displayed in the everyday actions of humanity, for "it is by his conduct and blessing, that all things come to pass."[86] He adds elsewhere, "As to his providences, wherein his sovereignty is also manifested; it is said, Zech. ii. 14. 'Be silent, O all flesh, before the Lord, for he is raised up out of his habitation.' It is spoken of his providential working in the changes of kingdoms and desolations that attend them."[87]

God's providential actions include formation and protection in the womb, the place and time of birth, the designation of family out of which one grows, the occasions and means of conversion, the employments in this world, marriage, children, daily provision of food and shelter, preservation from temptations of sin, prevention of spiritual dangers and miseries, and the bringing of His saints to their heavenly home.[88] But is God also absolutely sovereign over the suffering of humanity and, specifically, the suffering of the elect? To this question we now turn.

God's Sovereignty over Suffering

Flavel is consistent in his doctrine of divine sovereignty that God is in complete control over all things, including suffering. God is not only sovereign over all good things that happen, but also over all bad things, even the most severe sufferings that fall upon humanity. Flavel writes, "God's hand is to be acknowledged in the greatest afflictions that befal us."[89] At this point, we are not yet arguing why Flavel believed that God ordains suffering (chapter 4 examines this topic), but simply that Flavel believed that God does ordain it. He

---

85. Flavel, *Divine Conduct*, 4:347.
86. Flavel, *Seaman's Farewell*, 5:350.
87. Flavel, *Token for Mourners*, 5:627.
88. Flavel outlines each of these in detail in *Divine Conduct*, 4:342–412.
89. Flavel, *Exposition of the Assembly's Catechism*, 6:161.

exhorts his suffering reader, "Lift up thine eyes to the sovereign, wise, and holy pleasure that ordered this affliction."[90] Not only does Flavel explicitly argue that "afflictions [are] from the hand of God" and that God "is pleased to cast his own people into the fire of affliction,"[91] but he also assumes this premise throughout his writings as he unpacks various reasons God would ordain suffering.

Flavel believed that God brings affliction to both the believer and the unbeliever: "God gives the cup of affliction into the hands of the wicked"[92] and "hath seen it fit to set all his people in a state of trial in this world."[93] Elsewhere, he writes: "The rod of affliction goes round, and visits all sorts of persons, without difference; it is upon the tabernacles of the just and the unjust, the righteous and the wicked both are mourning under the rod."[94] However, he explains, "All sorts of outward afflictions are incident to all sorts of men.... Religion secures us from the *wrath*, but it does not secure us from the *rod* of God.... Surely none serve him *in vain* but those that serve him *vainly*. Godliness cannot secure you from affliction, but it can and will secure you from hell, and sanctify your afflictions to help you to heaven."[95]

The phrase used throughout his writings to indicate God's sovereignty over affliction is God's "afflictive providences."[96] Over and over again, Flavel couples affliction with God's providential design for affliction. He exhorts his reader, "O look to the hand of God in all, and know, that neither your comforts nor afflictions do arise out of the dust, or spring up out of the ground!"[97]

According to Flavel, nothing happens by chance, neither comfort nor affliction. God ordains the parameters of a person's life span,

---

90. Flavel, *Token for Mourners*, 5:627.
91. Flavel, *Touchstone of Sincerity*, 5:583.
92. Flavel, *Touchstone of Sincerity*, 5:544.
93. Flavel, *Touchstone of Sincerity*, 5:535.
94. Flavel, *Token for Mourners*, 5:623.
95. Flavel, *Balm of the Covenant*, 6:91.
96. For a sampling of these, see Flavel, *A Practical Treatise of Fear*, 3:316; *England's Duty*, 4:245; *Divine Conduct*, 4:407, 426, 433, 435, 460, 461.
97. Flavel, *Divine Conduct*, 4:464.

which "by his own counsel and will [God] hath allotted to every individual person."[98] Or, again, "It is God that *builds* and destroys families; he enlargeth and straiteneth them.... By their death, when God lops off the hopeful springing branches thereof."[99] The believer, in particular, is to be assured by the knowledge of God's sovereignty over suffering. He writes, "Let the assured soul be cast into what condition the Lord pleases; be it upon a bed of sickness" or "into a prison."[100] Flavel believed that God was completely sovereign over all afflictions: "Troubles and afflictions are of the Lord's framing and devising." Flavel explains that the believer should especially note God's "sovereignty, in electing the instruments of your affliction; in making them as afflictive as he pleaseth."[101]

In addition, God sets the boundaries for suffering. In drawing a metaphor between afflictions and a violent sea, Flavel writes, "When I see it threaten the shore with its proud, furious, and insulting waves, I wonder it doth not swallow up all: but I see it no sooner touch the sands, which God hath made its bounds, but it retires, and, as it were, with a kind of submission, respects those limits which God hath set it."[102] With those who would seek to harm and bring about suffering upon others, God "powerfully restrains creatures by the bridle of providence, from the commission of those things, to which their hearts are propense enough.... Jesus Christ limits the creatures in their acting, assigning them their boundaries and lines of liberty."[103]

That God is sovereign over all suffering also includes the suffering experienced by God's own Son, Jesus Christ. According to Flavel,

---

98. Flavel, *Token for Mourners*, 5:630. He also writes, "And let none say the death of children is a premature death. God hath ways to ripen them for heaven, whom he intends to gather thither betimes, the which we know not: in respect of fitness, they die in a full age, though they be cut off in the bud of their time." He adds later, "It is well for us and ours that our times are in God's hand, and not in our own." *Token for Mourners*, 5:630, 634.
99. Flavel, *Balm of the Covenant*, 6:91.
100. Flavel, *Sacramental Meditations*, 6:453.
101. Flavel, *Fountain of Life*, 1:364.
102. Flavel, *Navigation Spiritualized*, 5:254.
103. Flavel, *Fountain of Life*, 1:214.

the death of Christ was not by chance or accident but by design and appointment, so that "it was done according to the determinate counsel of God."[104] Jesus was "given by the Father" to be an atoning sacrifice for the elect. It was God who delivered Him "into the hands of justice to be punished."[105] To "the very torments of hell was Christ delivered, and that by the hand of his own Father."[106] The suffering of Christ did not escape the sovereign design and plan of God. Similarly, according to Flavel, that Christ was exalted and raised to life "imports the sovereignty and supremacy of Christ over all."[107] Christ, who suffered and died according to God's sovereign hand, was raised to life and now reigns and rules as the eternal Son of God.

It should be particularly noted that Flavel understood God's sovereignty to preside over every detail of suffering that comes upon the elect.[108] Every detail of time, place, and experience of suffering is divinely ordered so that it works out as God's unfolding plan of salvation history. Flavel explains:

> Now, every affliction that befals God's covenanted people, being placed by the most wise and infinite counsel of God in that very order, time, and manner in which they befal them, this very affliction, and not that, at this very time, and not at another, (it being always a time of need, 1 Pet. i. 6.) and ushered in by such forerunning occasions and circumstances: it must follow, that they all take the proper places, and come exactly at the fittest seasons; and if one of them were wanting, something would be defective in the frame of your happiness. As they now stand, they work together for your good, which displaced, they would not do.[109]

---

104. Acts 2:23, quoted in Flavel, *Fountain of Life*, 1:65.
105. Flavel, *Fountain of Life*, 1:65.
106. Flavel, *Fountain of Life*, 1:67.
107. Flavel, *Fountain of Life*, 1:518.
108. We will examine the different purposes of suffering for the Christian and for the non-Christian in chapter 4.
109. Flavel, *Balm of the Covenant*, 6:100.

As seen here, Flavel believes that God intentionally chooses every affliction that comes upon the believer. It is also important to note from this passage that suffering is to be understood as something "good" for the believer. Flavel asserts that the suffering that comes upon the Christian is a "sovereign cordial."[110] It comes "not merely from [God's] pleasure, but for our profit, that these breaches are made upon our families and comforts."[111] God's sovereignty over affliction, then, is expressed in His providence by bringing to fruition the actual suffering—in all its details—upon humanity.

To summarize, then, Flavel clearly taught that all affliction and suffering comes only by the hand and design of God: "In all the sad and afflictive providences that befal you, eye God as the author and orderer of them."[112] Not only has God decreed all the events and actions that take place in the course of time, but He also "rules and orders the kingdom of Providence, by supporting, permitting, restraining, limiting, protecting, punishing, and rewarding those over whom he reigns providentially"[113]—suffering included.

Sovereignty and the "Problem" of Evil

Before we leave this study of Flavel's understanding of sovereignty, we must address an obvious and important question as to the reality of God's sovereignty and the problem and presence of evil or, as it is often called, *theodicy*. These questions surround the issue of theodicy: If God truly governs and orders all humanity's actions, does that mean that He causes people to sin as well? Moreover, is God the author of evil as it is expressed in the actions of humanity? Flavel answers by arguing that providence is exercised with relation to sinful actions by "permitting them," "restraining them," and "overruling them to good."[114] He quotes Genesis 50:20, "But as for you, ye thought evil against me; but God meant it unto good." Nothing

---

110. Flavel, *Balm of the Covenant*, 6:113.
111. Flavel, *Balm of the Covenant*, 6:113.
112. Flavel, *Divine Conduct*, 4:426.
113. Flavel, *Fountain of Life*, 1:213.
114. Flavel, *Exposition of the Assembly's Catechism*, 6:165.

happens outside of God's sovereign control, including evil. But Flavel is careful not to assign evil to God. Rather, God permits it, restrains it, and overrules it—for His glory and the good of His people.

As we have seen, Flavel calls suffering the "fruit of sin" and distinguishes the types of evil involved with it. He explains how God cannot be the author of evil by way of explaining the exact nature of suffering: "Afflictions in themselves are evil, Amos ii. 6. very bitter and unpleasant. Yet not morally and intrinsically evil, as sin is; for if so, the holy God would never own it for his own act as he doth, Mic. iii. 2. but always disclaimeth sin. Besides, if it were so evil, it could, in no case or respect, be the object of our election and desire, as in some cases it ought to be, Heb. xi. 25. but it is evil, as it is the fruit of sin, and grievous unto sense."[115] Flavel argues in this section that while suffering is "an evil" in the sense that it is unpleasant, it is not "evil" in the sense of being intrinsically immoral. Otherwise, Flavel contends, God would not ordain it because He is holy. Thus Flavel calls afflictions that are used by God in the lives of the elect "sanctified afflictions."[116] Conversely, afflictions that are used by God in the lives of unbelievers are called "unsanctified afflictions."[117]

The only way in which afflictions may be "sanctified" in the life of the Christian is through the affliction of Christ on his or her behalf: "A sanctified affliction is a cup, whereinto Jesus hath wrung and pressed the juice and virtue of all his mediatorial offices."[118] The suffering toward the believer comes, not as punishment, but as fatherly discipline—what Flavel calls the "fruits of God's fatherly love."[119] Behind, or prior to, God's use of this first type of evil—as "affliction"—is its root in sin. While sin first brought affliction into the world, eternal affliction was taken out of the world by the affliction of Christ for all who receive Him as Savior and Lord.[120]

---

115. Flavel, *Navigation Spiritualized*, 5:251.
116. Flavel, *Navigation Spiritualized*, 5:251.
117. Flavel, *Navigation Spiritualized*, 5:252.
118. Flavel, *Navigation Spiritualized*, 5:252.
119. Flavel, *Navigation Spiritualized*, 5:252.
120. Flavel, *Navigation Spiritualized*, 5:253.

Flavel contends that the way in which we must understand the apparent problem of the coexistence of God's sovereignty and the presence of evil is that God permits evil for His glory and praise while remaining unstained by the corruption of it. Flavel writes, "[God] permits and suffers the worst of creatures in his dominion, to be and act as they do."[121] Expecting the natural objection, Flavel continues with theological precision: "Say not, that it is unbecoming the most Holy to permit such evils, which he could prevent if he pleased. For as he permits no more than he will over-rule to his praise, so that very permission of his, is holy and just."[122] Stating it positively, God permits evil. Stating it negatively, God withholds the restraints of evil. Either way, Flavel argues, God remains holy, and those who act out with evil are not "excused by his permissions of them."[123]

While God sovereignly decrees and orders evil, those decrees "are most pure, and altogether unspotted of sin."[124] He explains, "If [God] had plunged me into the sea of sorrow, yet I could say in all that sea of sorrow, there is not a drop of injustice."[125] While God ordains suffering, He remains holy and righteous. The believer expressing his faith will praise God in the midst of his suffering: "A gracious heart cleaves nearer and nearer to God in affliction, and can justify God in his severe strokes, acknowledging them to be all just and holy."[126]

The evil of affliction is the effect of sin. God permits and orders it to His praise and glory, but does so without being the "author" of evil. By permitting it, He withholds the restraints of the evil inclinations and propensities of humanity's sinful hearts and actions. In this way, He so governs evil for ultimate good: "But as for you, ye thought evil against me, but God meant it unto good."[127]

---

121. Flavel, *Fountain of Life*, 1:214. See also *Touchstone of Sincerity*, 5:551.
122. Flavel, *Fountain of Life*, 1:214.
123. Flavel, *Fountain of Life*, 1:214.
124. Flavel, *Exposition of the Assembly's Catechism*, 6:161.
125. Flavel, *Token for Mourners*, 5:605.
126. Flavel, *Token for Mourners*, 5:620.
127. Genesis 50:20, quoted in Flavel, *Exposition of the Assembly's Catechism*, 6:165.

To summarize, then, the sovereignty of God is displayed in both eternal decree and temporal providence. God's decrees are from all eternity, while His providences are the effectual application of those decrees in time and space. Therefore, providence and decree in Flavel's theology are the premises of his assumption of divine sovereignty. As sovereignty is an incommunicable attribute of God, decree and providence are the outworking of that particular attribute. All things, all actions, all events, and all people exist only by and under the sovereignty of God. That they exist is by His eternal decree, effectually brought forth in time and space by His providential governing.

That God is sovereign, according to Flavel, does not negate the responsibility of humanity. While God remains absolutely sovereign, man remains responsible. This is one of the reasons, as we have seen, why Flavel explicitly refers to divine conduct. Flavel's understanding of sovereignty is relational and actual, and is displayed in harmony with His imminence and omnipresence—which is why he stresses providence as the personal outworking of sovereignty in everyday life. Therefore, while Flavel supports God's "absolute sovereignty," he does not venture into a deistic, impersonal theology of God's control over history.

In addition, Flavel maintains a continuity and consistency in his theology of sovereignty when he addresses suffering. God not only ordains and governs all comforts and joys in this life, He also ordains and governs all discomforts and afflictions as well. Flavel argues that both are from God's sovereign hand. Can God, then, be found "guilty" of evil? Again, Flavel answers in the negative. While He permits the evil we see in the course of history, He remains holy, righteous, and unstained by it. The affliction in the world is an "evil" effect of sin. God, then, may permit and govern evil without being the "author" of evil. In no way, Flavel maintains, does the presence of evil detract from God's sovereignty or holiness.

Throughout his *Works*, Flavel consistently maintains a doctrine of the absolute sovereignty of God, displayed in decree and providence. This doctrine incorporates gospel themes, especially the atonement of Christ's death on the cross. That death, being by the sovereign plan and design of God, became the affliction that would conquer the eternal affliction for all the elect. The judgment that they deserved was placed upon Christ, so that Flavel calls any affliction they experience in this life "sanctified affliction." It is to God's purposes in ordaining suffering that we now turn.

CHAPTER FOUR

Flavel on God's Purposes in Ordaining Suffering

Flavel weaves together two theological-pastoral strands as part of his writing ministry to sufferers: (1) his understanding of why God ordains suffering and (2) how Christian sufferers ought to respond to their suffering. We will examine the first strand in this chapter and the second strand in the next.

For the Glory of God, the Good of the Elect, and the Judgment of the Wicked

In *Providence in Early Modern England*, Alexandra Walsham writes of the general Puritan understanding of suffering as "such 'crosses' and 'stripes' [with which] the Lord tenderly nurtured and disciplined His dearest children."[1] This understanding, of course, is from the vantage point of the believer in Christ. Walsham continues, "Hardship and disaster could also be compared with the furnace in which a potter tested his clay vessel, the crucible in which a goldsmith refined and 'skoured' precious metals. They were a form of trial by fire by which the Lord purged and proved His own. God afflicted the elect in this world that they might escape perdition in the next."[2] As we shall see in this chapter, the same conclusion may be found in Flavel's theology. It should be emphasized again that Flavel, like his Puritan contemporaries, did not see the study of sovereignty or suffering apart from its pastoral and practical implications. Where

---

1. Walsham, *Providence in Early Modern England*, 16.
2. Walsham, *Providence in Early Modern England*, 16.

he speaks of these topics in his *Works*, he speaks of them within the context of his greater ministry goals; namely, the glory of God and the ultimate good of His people. Flavel writes of God's design for suffering: "We must conclude, in the general, [God] certainly designs his own glory, and his people's advantage and profit in them."[3] Similarly, he writes, "The Lord gives them up into the hands of their enemies for the correction of their evils, and the manifestation of his own glory."[4]

Flavel maintains this eye toward God's glory in suffering, which gives greater weight to his position that there is no contradiction between the presence of suffering and the twofold goal of its bringing glory to God as well as ultimate good to His people: "Hereby the most wise God doth illustrate the glory of his own name, clearing up the righteousness of his ways by the sufferings of his own people. By this the word shall see, that how well soever he loves them, he will not indulge or patronize their sins; if they will be so disingenuous to abuse his favours, he will be so just to make them suffer for their sins, and by those very sufferings will provide for his own glory, which was by them clouded in the eyes of the world."[5]

At the same time—although it might seem ironic to say so—God increases the ultimate joy of believers by suffering. Flavel explains, "As God provides for his own glory, by the sufferings and troubles of his people; so he advanceth their happiness, and greatly promotes their interest thereby."[6] Moreover, God's glory and human suffering are not separated, but held together so that "when the Lord sees these sweet effects of his trial upon them, it greatly pleaseth him."[7] This is not to be understood in a sadistic

---

3. Flavel, *Touchstone of Sincerity*, 5:579. Similarly, he contends, "How many trials soever God brings his people under, to be sure neither his own glory nor their interest shall suffer any damage by them." *Touchstone of Sincerity*, 5:580.
4. Flavel, *Preparation for Sufferings*, 6:7.
5. Flavel, *Preparation for Sufferings*, 6:9.
6. Flavel, *Preparation for Sufferings*, 6:10.
7. Flavel, *Touchstone of Sincerity*, 5:582.

sense, but in a way that brings God glory and His people good. This is why Flavel can also write, "The mercies and compassions of God over his people are exceeding great and tender.... He delights not in afflicting and grieving them."[8] Thus Flavel's reasons for why God would ordain suffering are situated within the context of his desire to minister to, comfort, and console the sufferer, as well as his desire to encourage the afflicted to respond to suffering in a way that glorifies God.[9]

It is for this reason that Flavel sees the affliction of the saints as "sanctified afflictions."[10] These are sufferings brought about by the sovereign will and design of God in accordance with one of His many purposes for the saints—all of them, to be sure, for their ultimate good: "And so for afflictions of all kinds, the greatest and sorest of them; they do work, by the influence of providence, a great deal of good to the saints, and that not only as the occasions, but as the instruments and means of it…by the instrumentality of this sanctified affliction."[11] From the standpoint of the elect, these afflictions are "sanctified, sweetened, and turned into blessings."[12] Afflictive providences, then, "are blessings to [believers], and come from the love of God."[13] The opposite, however, is true for the unbeliever. God gives all people—believer and unbeliever alike—signs

---

8. Flavel, *Preparation for Sufferings*, 6:7. Even when executing judgment, "[God] delays the execution as long as the honour of his name and safety of his people will permit."

9. With particular reference, Flavel notes that he seeks to "apply myself to the work of counselling and comforting the afflicted." *Token for Mourners*, 5:626.

10. Flavel frequently speaks of suffering by this designation; see *Divine Conduct*, 4:407–8; *Navigation Spiritualized*, 5:218, 251–52. As we have observed, he sees affliction within God's sovereign will for humanity.

11. Flavel, *Divine Conduct*, 4:478.

12. Flavel, *Navigation Spiritualized*, 5:218. Similarly, he writes, "Consider your spiritual mercies and privileges with which the Lord Jesus hath invested you, and repine at your lot of providence if you can. One of these mercies alone, hath enough in it to sweeten all your troubles in this world." *Divine Conduct*, 4:432.

13. Flavel, *Divine Conduct*, 4:480.

of His coming judgment, which shall be executed in full upon the unbeliever. In writing of the decay of life, death, calamity, plague, and other afflictions that come upon people, Flavel explains: "When such symptoms of God's indignation do appear upon any people, the Lord, by them...forewarns the world that his judgments are near."[14] Thus, sufferings serve to warn the faithless of greater judgment to come.

We may summarize one of Flavel's propositions at this point: While affliction and suffering come upon the unbeliever as signs and effects of God's judgment and wrath, they come upon the elect as loving discipline with a design to produce greater godliness. The only reason for the change in the goal of each particular suffering is whether it has been "sanctified" through Christ's sacrifice of atonement. Flavel explains, "The reason why [afflictions] become thus sweet and pleasant is, because they run now in another channel; Jesus Christ hath removed them from mount Ebal to Gerizim; they are no more the effects of vindictive wrath, but paternal chastisement."[15] Only through Christ, then, can suffering turn to blessing, which means that this can only be true for the Christian. It is only through "the efficacy and virtue of Christ's blood" that "sanctified afflictions...produce such blessed effects upon the soul."[16] He adds this important definition: "Behold, then, a sanctified affliction is a cup, whereinto Jesus hath wrung and pressed the juice and virtue of all his mediatorial offices. Surely, that must be a cup of generous, royal wine, like that in the supper, a cup of blessing to the people of God."[17] For the elect, affliction should not "be interpreted as a mark or sign of God's hatred or enmity." Rather, [God's] heart is full of love, whilst the face of providence is full of frowns."[18]

---

14. Flavel, *Preparation for Sufferings*, 6:15.
15. Flavel, *Navigation Spiritualized*, 5:252.
16. Flavel, *Divine Conduct*, 4:408. Similarly, he writes, "Sanctified afflictions working under the efficacy of the blood of Christ, are the safest way to our souls." *Treatise of the Soul of Man*, 2:151.
17. Flavel, *Navigation Spiritualized*, 5:252.
18. Flavel, *Divine Conduct*, 4:429.

Flavel concerns himself throughout his *Works* with ministering to the believer in Christ rather than to the unbeliever. Afflictions are not "sanctified" for the unbeliever, but rather come as raw effects of God's wrath. Flavel argues that unbelievers "are prejudiced and hardened" by affliction. "However, therein God accomplishes his word, and executeth his decree."[19] Moreover, Flavel admits that his words have little to no comfort for the unregenerate.[20] He explains, "As the worst things are ordered to the benefit of the saints, so the best things wicked men enjoy do them no good."[21] For the elect, suffering comes to accomplish one (or more) of many God-ordained purposes—for His glory and their ultimate good.

Due to Flavel's primary concern with writing to his fellow Christians, this chapter codifies eight general categories of Flavel's understanding of the reasons for which God ordains suffering for the elect: (1) to reveal, deter, and mortify sin; (2) to produce godliness and spiritual fruit; (3) to reveal the character of God; (4) to relinquish the temporal for the eternal; (5) to produce a sincere faith, devoid of hypocrisy; (6) to encourage fellowship with God through Word, prayer, and sacrament; (7) to bear witness to the world; and (8) to cultivate greater communion with Christ, the greatest sufferer. The goal of the remaining portion of this chapter, then, is to examine Flavel's answer to the question of why God ordains suffering.

To Reveal, Deter, and Mortify Sin

Flavel writes that God ordains suffering for the threefold purpose of showing the believer his sin, of deterring or preventing the believer

---

19. Flavel, *Touchstone of Sincerity*, 5:580. He explains elsewhere, "Put all afflictions, calamities, sufferings, and miseries of this world into one scale, and this sentence of God into the other, and they will be all lighter than a feather." *Method of Grace*, 2:435.

20. Flavel, *Token for Mourners*, 5:624. Even still, God does provide various means by His common grace to alleviate their sorrow in this life. See *Token for Mourners*, 5:624.

21. Flavel, *Divine Conduct*, 4:478–79. He adds, "As persons are, so things work for good or evil."

from sinning, and of mortifying sin in his life. By ordaining various sufferings in the believer's life, "God is but killing your lusts, weaning your hearts from a vain world, preventing temptations, and exciting desires after heaven."[22] There is both a negative and positive purpose in dealing with sin, though they are two sides of the same coin. Negatively, God ordains suffering to reveal, deter, and mortify sin. Positively, God ordains suffering to produce godliness and awaken the soul to produce greater "spiritual fruit." Flavel explains, "Mortification of our sinful affections and passions, is the one half of our sanctification, Rom. vi. 11. 'Dead indeed unto sin, but alive unto God.'"[23] Sanctification, then, is the goal of these two halves so that believers are "purged and made more spiritual under the rod!"[24] The first half will be examined in this section, the second in the next.

To Reveal Sin
First, Flavel argues that God ordains suffering to reveal sin. He writes, "Sometimes the Lord sanctifies afflictions to discover the corruption that is in the heart.... When a sharp affliction comes, then the pride, impatience, and unbelief of the heart appear."[25] Even the slightest sufferings can reveal "much falseness, rottenness, pride, and selfishness in the heart."[26] Or, again, "Such sufferings as these will discover the falseness and rottenness of men's hearts."[27]

When sufferings press against an individual, he or she may see his or her true inclinations, which, Flavel believes, are often full of

---

22. Flavel, *Divine Conduct*, 4:429.
23. Flavel, *Divine Conduct*, 4:405.
24. Flavel, *Touchstone of Sincerity*, 5:579.
25. Flavel, *Navigation Spiritualized*, 5:251. He explains elsewhere, "Ah! little did I think, saith one, that I had so much love for the world, and so little for God, until afflictions tried it. I could not have believed that ever the creature had got so deep into my heart, until providence either threatened or made a separation, and then I found it. I thought I had been rich in faith, until such a danger befel me, or such a want began to pinch hard; and then I saw how unable I was to trust God for protection, or provision." *Touchstone of Sincerity*, 5:581.
26. Flavel, *Touchstone of Sincerity*, 5:587.
27. Flavel, *Touchstone of Sincerity*, 5:575.

sin. In this way, the sinner is able more and more to see the depths of sin in his or her own heart. Flavel writes, "I heartily wish that these searching afflictions may make the more satisfying discoveries; that you may now see more of the evil of sin, the vanity of the creature, and the fulness of Christ, than ever you yet saw. Afflictions are searchers, and put the soul upon searching and trying its ways, Lam. iii. 14. When our sin finds us out by affliction, happy are we, if, by the light of affliction we find out sin."[28] These "searching afflictions" are meant to reveal sin to the sinner so that they might both deter him or her from transgressing further and mortify the very sin that has been exposed. Flavel's desire is to guide his reader to understand that suffering is a revealing blessing: "If the Lord would but strike in with this affliction, and by it open thine eyes to see thy deplorable state."[29] Suffering opens the eyes of faith to see one's own sin, providing a foundation for both deterring and mortifying that sin.

To Deter Sin

Second, Flavel maintains that God ordains suffering to deter or to prevent the believer from committing even greater sins. God will often lay "some strong afflictions on the body, to prevent a worse evil."[30] Sufferings work upon believers' hearts "to restrain them from sin, or warn them against sin."[31] One of the ways this goal of suffering "works" is by making adversity strong where sin is strong. Thus he can write, "[God] had rather their hearts should be heavy under adversity, than vain and careless under prosperity; the choicest spirits have been exercised with the sharpest sufferings."[32] God's preserving of His people by preventing them from committing greater sin is a distinct goal noted in Flavel's theology of

---

28. Flavel, *Token for Mourners*, 5:605–6.
29. Flavel, *Token for Mourners*, 5:625.
30. Flavel, *Divine Conduct*, 4:400. He calls this goal of affliction a "preservative from sin."
31. Flavel, *Divine Conduct*, 4:407. See also *Touchstone of Sincerity*, 5:580 and *Divine Conduct*, 4:429, 437.
32. Flavel, *Preparation for Sufferings*, 6:7.

suffering: "[Sufferings] come in a proper season, when we have need of them, either to prevent some sin we are falling into, or recover us out of a remiss, supine, and careless frame of spirit into which we are fallen.... These providences speak the jealousy of God over us, and his care to prevent far worse evils by these sad, but needful strokes."[33] In this way—by causing troubles as the effect of sin—afflictions "turn our hearts against sin." Suffering, therefore, is a deterrent from committing greater sin because the sufferer is shown the devastating effects of his or her sin and the heaviness with which he bears under the weight of his sin. "Afflictions," Flavel adds, "are used by God…to stop the gaps and keep you from breaking out of God's way."[34]

To Mortify Sin
The third and primary way in which God negatively deals with sin in the believer, Flavel contends, is by ordaining suffering to mortify sin. Flavel writes, "These troubles are ordered as so many occasions and means to mortify the corruptions that are in their hearts.... Adversity kills those corruptions which prosperity bred."[35] From this last line, we may see Flavel's thought that God sends suffering so that the believer might not make an idol of God's creation. In other words, Flavel wants his reader to see the danger of elevating the gifts of this world above the Giver of worldly things, which he calls idolatry. In connecting this to Christ, he explains, "The intent of the Redeemer's undertaking was not to produce for his people riches, ease, and pleasures on earth; but to mortify their lusts, heal their natures, and spiritualize their affections; and thereby to fit them for the eternal fruition of God."[36] Thus to mortify a worldly affection by causing suffering is to mortify sin. Flavel maintains that earthly pleasures get in the way of godliness and so God ordains suffering to wean believers from the vanity of worldly possessions.

---

33. Flavel, *Divine Conduct*, 4:480.
34. Flavel, *Fountain of Life*, 1:554.
35. Flavel, *Preparation for Sufferings*, 6:10.
36. Flavel, *Balm of the Covenant*, 6:84.

In a similar vein, Flavel urges his readers to ascribe honor to God alone. Otherwise, the temptations that befall humanity quickly plunge them into greater sin. The solution is that God mortifies a misdirected honor and, therefore, the pollution of sin. Flavel explains, "The design and aim of these afflictive providences, is to purge and cleanse them from that pollution into which temptations have plunged them."[37] Flavel sees these afflictions as "cleansers," which "pull down pride, refine the earthliness, and purge out the vanity of the spirit."[38] He writes, "Sanctified afflictions are cleansers and purgers too."[39] Particularly, the sins of "pride and self-confidence are destroyed and mortified in the saints."[40] Pride is directly opposed to God and therefore is mortified by a humbling experience such as suffering. "How hath God blessed crosses to mortify corruption, wants to kill our wantonness, disappointments to wean us from the world!"[41] To mortify sin, Flavel contends, is a primary reason God ordains suffering.

It should be noted that Flavel does not believe that affliction—in and of itself—has power to mortify sin. He explains, "No afflictions, how many, or strong, or continual soever they be, can in themselves purge away the pollution of sin."[42] This is why Flavel argues that there is a difference between a sanctified affliction and an unsanctified affliction: "A sanctified affliction may, in the efficacy and virtue of Christ's blood, produce blessed effects upon the soul."[43] How is

---

37. Flavel, *Divine Conduct*, 4:407. Similarly, he writes, "By your afflictions, your corruptions are not only clogged, but purged." *Fountain of Life*, 1:555. Perhaps more directly, he writes, "Sanctified afflictions are ordered and prescribed in heaven for the purging of our corruptions." *Method of Grace*, 2:390.

38. Flavel, *Divine Conduct*, 4:481. He also writes, "It is a sure sign afflicting providences are sanctified when they purge the heart from sin, and leave both heart and life more pure, heavenly, mortified, and humble than they found them."

39. Flavel, *Fountain of Life*, 1:555. See also *Treatise of the Soul of Man*, 2:113.

40. Flavel, *Touchstone of Sincerity*, 5:581.

41. Flavel, *Divine Conduct*, 4:442.

42. Flavel, *Divine Conduct*, 4:407.

43. Flavel, *Divine Conduct*, 4:407.

this realized in the life of the believer? "Christ cures troubles, by *sanctifying* them to the souls of his that are under affliction, and makes their troubles *medicinal* and healing to them."[44] Suffering remains only and necessarily dreadful in its end and goal unless "Christ's sanctifying hand and art have passed upon them."[45] When this happens, "they are no more the effects of vindictive wrath, but paternal chastisement."[46] In other words, God's purpose that suffering mortify sin only works toward that end in those for whom the blood of Christ has already made atonement. In the end, the mortification of sin by affliction turns the believer toward Christ with greater affection. This greater affection for Christ then gives greater strength to endure suffering. Flavel explains, "It is the strength of our affections that puts so much strength into our afflictions."[47]

To Produce Godliness and Spiritual Fruit

As Flavel argues that the negative side of the sanctification process is to reveal, deter, and mortify sin, so also he argues that the positive side of sanctification is to produce godliness and spiritual fruit. Not only does sin need to be removed, it also needs to be replaced by those things that are pleasing to God. It is not enough for sin to be dealt with, leaving the individual with some sort of blank slate. The fruit of the Spirit must replace sin.[48]

Flavel explains that there must be a radical shift in the way one understands happiness, especially the happiness of believers. Happiness comes not by possessing earthly treasure, prosperity, titles, or ease. Rather, happiness comes by pleasing God. Flavel explains, "As God provides for his own glory, by the sufferings and troubles of his people; so he advanceth their happiness, and greatly promotes their

---

44. Flavel, *Method of Grace*, 2:194.
45. Flavel, *Navigation Spiritualized*, 5:252.
46. Flavel, *Navigation Spiritualized*, 5:252.
47. Flavel, *Practical Treatise of Fear*, 3:295.
48. Taken from Galatians 5:22–23, these include love, joy, peace, patience, kindness, goodness, faithfulness, gentleness, and self-control.

interest thereby."⁴⁹ This "interest" of the church is shored up and promoted by "a suffering condition."⁵⁰

When believers please God by faith-filled good works, they are filled with happiness and bring glory to God. This, then, is the church's glory—to exhibit a reflection of God's communicable attributes. Suffering is the ground from which God brings forth this glory of the church. Flavel writes, "If you reckon [the church's] glory to consist in its humility, faith, patience, and heavenly-mindedness, no condition in the world abounds with advantages for these, as an afflicted condition doth. It was not persecutions and prisons, but worldliness and wantonness, that was the poison of the church."⁵¹ He adds more directly, "The power of godliness did never thrive better than in affliction."⁵² Suffering, then, is the breeding ground of spiritual fruit so that God plants the believer, as it were, into the soil of suffering to produce godliness.

When Christians suffer, they suffer so as to bring glory to God through the increase of their own godliness, which is the process of sanctification. In sanctification, believers are refined through suffering to produce godliness. When Christians are dealt "afflictions from the hand of God," Flavel explains, *"Here is the faith and patience of the saints;* here is there courage, meekness, and self-denial, shining as gold in the fire."⁵³

In addition to these fruits of the Spirit produced in the individual believer, Flavel maintains that, by affliction, the church as

---

49. Flavel, *Preparation for Sufferings*, 6:10.
50. Flavel, *Preparation for Sufferings*, 6:10.
51. Flavel, *A Saint Indeed*, 5:448. Similarly, he writes, "And, certainly, if we reckon humility, heavenly mindedness, contempt of the world, and longing desires after heaven, to be the real interest and advantage of the church; then it is evident nothing so much promotes their interest, as a suffering condition doth." *Preparation for Sufferings*, 6:10.
52. Flavel, *A Saint Indeed*, 5:448.
53. Flavel, *Touchstone of Sincerity*, 5:583. In writing of the death of a son, Flavel exhorts his reader to let the affliction produce gratitude for all that the Lord has left in his or her life. "Whatever God takes, be still thankful for what he leaves." *Token for Mourners*, 5:617.

a community is sanctified. He writes, "The church's sufferings are ordered and sanctified, to endear them to each other. Times of common suffering are times of reconciliation, and greater endearments among the people of God; never more endeared, than when most persecuted; never more united, than when most scattered."[54] By common sufferings, Flavel argues, believers enter into deeper and more meaningful fellowship with one another. This fellowship is heightened under "reproofs of the rod," too, because "they are humbled for their pride, wantonness, and bitterness of their spirits to each other."[55] By sufferings, God produces godliness in the individual believer as well as in the community of the church. Flavel explains, "The relation we sustain to God's afflicted people: they are members with us in one body, and the members should have the same care of one another."[56] This positive effect of the revealing, deterring, and mortifying of sin is part of God's design for the sanctification of the elect: "How cross soever the winds and tides of providence at any time seem to us, yet nothing is more certain, than that they all conspire to hasten sanctified souls to God, and fit them for glory."[57]

To Reveal the Character of God

As noted, Flavel understood that one part of God's purpose for suffering is to bring Himself glory. This means exhibiting something of His own character—the display of His manifold perfections. Flavel believed that one of the reasons God ordains suffering is to reveal His own attributes and character.[58] He writes, "Hereby the most wise God doth illustrate the glory of his own name, clearing up the righteousness of his ways by the sufferings of his people."[59]

---

54. Flavel, *Preparation for Sufferings*, 6:11.
55. Flavel, *Preparation for Sufferings*, 6:11.
56. Flavel, *Fountain of Life*, 1:245.
57. Flavel, *Divine Conduct*, 4:442.
58. This, Flavel believed, was also one of the reasons *Christ* suffered. He explains, "That in his sufferings there would be made a glorious display and manifestation of the divine attributes." *Sacramental Meditations*, 6:437.
59. Flavel, *Preparation for Sufferings*, 6:9.

God's glory, Flavel maintains, is displayed through suffering. His glory, as the sum total of His manifold attributes displayed, is seen by moving from the lesser to the greater. In other words, where one views by faith an act of God's mercy, it is part of His glory. So when a believer gives praise to God for one of His attributes, he is at the same time glorifying God.

This last element is an important aspect in understanding Flavel's theology of suffering. He sees the various attributes of God as an organically extended characteristic of His glory: "By exposing his people to such grievous sufferings, he gives a fit opportunity to manifest the glory of his power…and of his wisdom."[60] Suffering reveals the glory of God's manifold attributes, which is viewed by faith individually through particular afflictions. These attributes work together as a tapestry of His glory: "It is a pleasant sight to see the harmony of God's attributes."[61] While some attributes—such as mercy and justice—seem to contradict each other, Flavel holds all of God's attributes in a harmonious relationship. He explains, "Divine attributes…may seem sometimes to jar and clash to part with each other, and go contrary ways; but they only seem so to do, for in the winding up, they always meet, and embrace each other."[62] Here, then, is a sampling from Flavel's works of some of these divine attributes that God reveals through the suffering of His people:

- Wisdom: Flavel writes, "The wisdom of God is much seen in the choice of his rods."[63] "Eye the wisdom of God in all your afflictions, behold it in the choice of the kind of your affliction, this, and not another."[64] Flavel wants his reader to pay special attention to the kind of suffering that he or she undergoes. God does not cast arbitrary suffering upon His people.

---

60. Flavel, *Preparation for Sufferings*, 6:9–10.
61. Flavel, *Divine Conduct*, 4:440.
62. Flavel, *Divine Conduct*, 4:439.
63. Flavel, *Divine Conduct*, 4:480.
64. Flavel, *Divine Conduct*, 4:427. Similarly, he writes, "Behold the wisdom and goodness of God…by afflictions from the hand of God." *Touchstone of Sincerity*, 5:583. See also *Preparation for Sufferings*, 6:10; *Fountain of Life*, 1:222.

Rather, with great wisdom, He selects the type of suffering most profitable for His glory and His people's sanctification.

- Faithfulness: According to Flavel, God's faithfulness is seen in the midst of suffering: "Set the faithfulness of the Lord before you under the saddest providences."[65] "[God] took not up the rod to smite you, till his faithfulness and tender love to your souls called upon him to correct you."[66] When affliction comes knocking, Flavel exhorts his Christian readers to look upon God, who will neither leave them nor forsake them. He wants his readers to know that God will not suddenly turn His back upon His people in suffering. Rather, God remains faithful, and this knowledge should bring great hope to the suffering believer.

- Fatherly love: "As a father's hand correcting thee in love and faithfulness.... O if once you could but see affliction as a rod in a father's hand, proceeding from his love, and intended for your eternal good."[67] As a rod of love, affliction comes precisely because God loves His people. As a loving father will discipline his son, so also a loving God will discipline His people: "Hence also should gracious souls draw much encouragement and comfort amidst all their troubles. O these are the fruits of God's fatherly love."[68] Also, "His heart is full of love, whilst the face of providence is full of frowns."[69] Even though it may seem like the suffering

---

65. Flavel, *Divine Conduct*, 4:427. See also *Method of Grace*, 2:413. He writes, "The faithfulness of God is given by promise for his people's security in, and encouragement against all their suffering and afflictions in this world.... Believe it, Christians, the faithfulness of God runs through all his works of providence." *Righteous Man's Refuge*, 3:367.

66. Flavel, *Token for Mourners*, 5:649.

67. Flavel, *Token for Mourners*, 5:665. For examples of this, see *Divine Conduct*, 4:442, 480; *Token for Mourners*, 5:649; *A Saint Indeed*, 5:444, 448; *Method of Grace*, 2:247, 272; *Exposition of the Assembly's Catechism*, 6:310; *Fountain of Life*, 1:222; *Balm of the Covenant*, 6:105.

68. Flavel, *Navigation Spiritualized*, 5:252. See also *Righteous Man's Refuge*, 3:396.

69. Flavel, *Divine Conduct*, 4:429.

Flavel on God's Purposes in Ordaining Suffering   71

that befalls a Christian is an effect of hate, it comes from a heart of love.

- Goodness: Flavel is careful to point out and maintain the goodness of God in the midst of suffering: "Own and admire the bounty and goodness of God manifested to thee in this affliction."[70] He writes elsewhere, "Behold the wisdom and goodness of God…by afflictions from the hand of God."[71] Suffering comes from the hand of a good God who should not be charged with evil. Admiring the goodness of God in the midst of suffering is an expression of worship for the believer and, as such, brings honor to God.

- Grace and mercy: It almost seems like a paradox that Flavel sees God as revealing His grace and mercy when suffering comes upon the Christian. He writes, "This affliction for which thou mournest, may be the greatest mercy to thee that ever yet befel thee in this world."[72] "Set the *grace* and *goodness* of God before you in all afflictive providences; O see him passing by you in the cloudy and dark day, proclaiming his name, *the Lord, the Lord merciful and gracious*."[73] When suffering comes, it comes to make the Christian more holy and to save him or her from greater suffering—eternal suffering.

- Sovereignty: As God is morally and perfectly good, so also is He completely sovereign. Flavel explains, "Eye God in the whole process of the affliction…as a sovereign hand, which hath right to dispose of thee, and all thy comforts, without thy leave or consent."[74] "In all the sad and afflictive providences that befal you, eye God as the author and orderer of them also…. Set before you the *sovereignty* of God, eye him

---

70. Flavel, *Token for Mourners*, 5:624.
71. Flavel, *Touchstone of Sincerity*, 5:583. See also *Divine Conduct*, 4:426, 441.
72. Flavel, *Token for Mourners*, 5:625.
73. Flavel, *Divine Conduct*, 4:426–27. See also *Touchstone of Sincerity*, 5:581; *Token for Mourners*, 5:665; *Divine Conduct*, 4:442; and *Preparation for Sufferings*, 6:9.
74. Flavel, *Token for Mourners*, 5:664.

as being infinitely superior to you, at whose pleasure you, and all you have is."⁷⁵ According to Flavel, the suffering that comes upon a Christian is not by chance, but by the hand of a sovereign God. He has the free power and authority to dispense affliction upon humanity as He sees fit.

- Immutability: Flavel is clear that, while people change, God does not. He writes, "Eye the *immutability* of God; look on him as the rock of ages.... It may be two or three days have made a sad change in your condition: The death of a dear relation hath turned all things upside down.... O how composing are those views of God to our spirits under dark providences."⁷⁶ Even though life comes and goes, Flavel urges his reader to look upon the Rock unchanging for comfort and rest. To reveal His unchangeable character, God ordains suffering for His people.

- Just and righteous: Suffering is deserved, according to Flavel. There is not a speck of injustice in any amount of affliction that a person experiences: "[Eye God in affliction]...as a just and righteous hand. Hast not thou procured this to thyself by thy own folly? Yea, the Lord is just in all that is come upon thee; whatever he hath done, yet he hath done thee no wrong."⁷⁷

- All-sufficiency: God ordains suffering to show how empty and insufficient possessions and earthly treasures really are. The believer may enjoy earthly comforts, but he will always remain wanting if he does not see God as the greater and all-sufficient joy. Flavel explains, "Eye the *all-sufficiency* of

---

75. Flavel, *Divine Conduct*, 4:426. See also *Preparation for Sufferings*, 6:9; *Fountain of Life*, 1:222.

76. Flavel, *Divine Conduct*, 4:426–27. He explains elsewhere, "The unchangeable God hath secured his loving kindness to his people, by promise, under all the trials and smarting rods of affliction with which he chastens them in this world." *Righteous Man's Refuge*, 3:378.

77. Flavel, *Token for Mourners*, 5:665. Note that this is for the *believer*, not the unbeliever. As we examined above, God's justice and righteousness through affliction is seen in the effects of wrath and judgment for the unbeliever.

God in the day of affliction; see enough in him still whatever be gone"[78] and asks, "Doth it become the children of such a Father to distrust his all-sufficiency, or repine at any of his dispensations?"[79]

Indeed, Flavel sees a vast variety of attributes displayed through suffering. These listed here, and others—such as God's being patient with and jealous for His people, as well as their healer, rescuer, preserver, and deliverer[80]—all point to this singular reason that God ordains suffering: to reveal His divine character.

To Relinquish the Temporal for the Eternal

According to Flavel, a fourth reason God ordains suffering is to have the believer relinquish a hold on the temporal, worldly life and the things in it for the eternal, heavenly life. This can be organized in at least four distinct ways: (1) by loosening the believer's grip on temporal and earthly things; (2) by showing the believer the vanity of this world; (3) by revealing the true nature of comfort; and (4) by making the believer long for heaven.

To Loosen the Believer's Grip on Temporal and Earthly Things

This aspect of relinquishing the temporal for the eternal is closely aligned with what Flavel sees as God's mortifying sin through suffering. "Be careful to…mortify your inordinate affections to earthly things," Flavel writes. Rather, "exercise heavenly mindedness, and keep your hearts upon things eternal, under all the providences with which the Lord exercises you in this world."[81] Similarly, God has "blessed crosses to mortify corruption…and to wean us from the world!"[82]

---

78. Flavel, *Divine Conduct*, 4:427.
79. This is in context of Flavel's writing about afflictions or "straits." *A Saint Indeed*, 5:461.
80. See Flavel, *Token for Mourners*, 5:625; *Preparation for Sufferings*, 6:9–10; *Divine Conduct*, 4:480.
81. Flavel, *Divine Conduct*, 4:429–30.
82. Flavel, *Divine Conduct*, 4:442. For a similar thought, see *Fountain of Life*, 1:522–23; *England's Duty*, 4:135.

Flavel means for his reader to see the comparison between the fleeting, temporary pleasures of this world and the permanent ones of the next. His exhortation is that "by all your troubles, God hath been weaning you from the world…and drawing out your souls to a more excellent life and state than this."[83]

This reason for suffering is for the believer's sanctification and ultimate good, which Flavel, as mentioned above, sees as a "weaning" process. It is, he explains, "for the [saints'] advantage to be weaned from the love of, and delight in ensnaring worldly vanities! To be quickened, and pricked forward with more haste to heaven, to have clearer discoveries of their own hearts, to be taught to pray more fervently, frequently, spiritually: to look and long for the rest to come, more ardently."[84] The loosening of the believer's grip on earthly things—"to wean off your affections, and crucify them to the world"[85]—is a primary way in which he or she may take hold of heavenly and eternal things. Flavel adds, "Ah! little did I think, saith one, that I had so much love for the world, and so little for God, until afflictions tried it."[86]

To Reveal the Vanity of Earthly Things

God ordains suffering to reveal the vanity of earthly things. Flavel writes, "Sanctified afflictions discover the emptiness and vanity of the creature."[87] He puts it another way: "Thy affliction is a fair class to discover [the creature's vanity]; for the vanity of the creature is never so effectually and sensibly discovered, as in our own experience of it."[88] Part of the suffering as one experiences it, then, is

---

83. Flavel, *Fountain of Life*, 1:555.
84. Flavel, *A Saint Indeed*, 5:448. See also *Treatise of the Soul of Man*, 2:600.
85. Flavel, *Preparation for Sufferings*, 6:55. See also Flavel's exhortation: "Get a weaned heart from all earthly enjoyments. If the heart be inordinately fixed upon any one thing that you possess in the world, that inordinate estimation of, and affection for it, will strangely effeminate, soften, and cowardize your spirit when your trial comes." *Preparation for Sufferings*, 6:49.
86. Flavel, *Touchstone of Sincerity*, 5:581.
87. Flavel, *Navigation Spiritualized*, 5:251. See also *A Saint Indeed*, 5:448.
88. Flavel, *A Saint Indeed*, 5:443.

the despair of expecting great things of the creation only to be let down when it does not furnish one with promised happiness and joy. Through affliction, "God hath now made thy heart soft by trouble, shewed thee the vanity of this world, and what a poor trifle it is which though [sic] madest thy happiness."[89]

Flavel's pastoral concern is to help his reader find comfort in what is heavenly and eternal, not in those things that are earthly and temporal. He explains, "The corruption of the heart shews itself in raising up great expectations to ourselves from the creature, and projecting abundance of felicity and contentment from some promising and hopeful enjoyments we have in the world.... But how soon were all these expectations dashed by a gloomy providence that benighted him in the noon-tide of his prosperity; and all this for his good, to take off his heart more fully from creature expectations."[90] Through suffering, God reveals the vanity of placing comfort in earthly things so as to show the security and worthiness of placing one's comfort in heavenly and eternal things.

To Reveal the True Nature of Comfort
In line with this sense of true comfort, Flavel writes, "If God be your God, you have really lost nothing by the removal of any creature-comfort."[91] Why? Because "God is the fountain of all true comfort."[92] Flavel makes a distinction between false comfort and true comfort. False comfort is found by placing one's trust in the temporal, vain things of this world. True comfort, on the other hand, is found by placing one's trust in the unchanging God. Comfort, therefore, is closely connected to trusting that which is secure, lasting, and good. However, there is also a kind of comfort that is not "false"—meaning, placed in something vain—but only temporary. This type of comfort is not inherently sinful.

---

89. Flavel, *Token for Mourners*, 5:625.
90. Flavel, *Divine Conduct*, 4:409.
91. Flavel, *Token for Mourners*, 5:651.
92. Flavel, *Token for Mourners*, 5:651.

Flavel divides comfort into two types: "*natural* and *sensitive, divine* and *spiritual.*"[93] He adds, "There is a time when it becomes Christians to exercise both...and there is a time when the former is to be suspended and laid by." Thus, we see that the believer must realize that if he or she finds comfort in earthly or "natural" things, it is only temporary and not lasting. By contrast, "there is no season," Flavel responds, "wherein spiritual joy and comfort in God is unseasonable."[94]

Flavel understood that even "good" earthly things—such as "father, mother, wife, or child"—should not be the foundation of our comfort: "God hath better things to comfort his people with than these, and worse rods to afflict you with than the removal of these."[95] It is important to see that the primary reason that these comforts do not provide "true" comfort is that they do not last. He explains further, "Every comfortable enjoyment, whether it be in relations, estate, health, or friends, is a candle lighted by providence for our comforts in this world, and they are but candles, which will not always last.... It is a dark hour with us, when these comforts are put out."[96] The suffering of losing a loved one, as Flavel mentions here, is real and painful. But Flavel exhorts his reader to step back and take a big-picture view from heaven's perspective. This, again, is for God's glory and the believer's sanctification: "It is usual with God to smite us in those very comforts which stole away too much of the love and delight of our souls from God."[97] These "sanctified strokes" cause the believer to find less comfort in the fleeting things of this world and more comfort in the eternal things of the next.[98] As for the things in this world, Flavel writes, "For the love of this world, away with it, crucify it, crucify it: down with the idol."[99]

---

93. Flavel, *Divine Conduct*, 4:428.
94. Flavel, *Divine Conduct*, 4:428.
95. Flavel, *Token for Mourners*, 5:628.
96. Flavel, *Token for Mourners*, 5:645.
97. Flavel, *Divine Conduct*, 4:480.
98. Flavel, *Divine Conduct*, 4:480–81.
99. Flavel, *Preparation for Sufferings*, 6:54.

Flavel exhorts his reader to find ultimate joy and comfort in God so that when suffering comes, the believer will not ultimately be shaken and plagued by fear, despair, or sorrow. What is this "comfort in God"? Flavel explains, "This spiritual joy or comfort is nothing else but the cheerfulness of our heart in God, and the sense of our interest in him, and in his promises."[100] Thus comfort in God is closely connected with the believer's assurance, a topic we will examine in the next chapter. A believer's comfort and assurance of salvation are inexorably linked: "*Faith* may be separated from comfort, but assurance cannot."[101] That is why Flavel sees suffering as a way to pry one's comfort from the temporal and attach it to the eternal—so that he or she may find assurance in the eternal rather than the temporal.[102]

To Make the Believer Long for Heaven

Finally, the last part of this reason for suffering, of having the believer relinquish the temporal for the eternal, can be seen in Flavel's argument that suffering makes the believer long for heaven. The believer, he explains, should rest also in the fact that God will save His elect no matter what amount of worldly possessions they may attain. But the loss of possessions points our thoughts and affections heavenward, for God "would never give you so much of the world to lose your hearts in the love of it, or so little to distract you with the cares of it."[103] He adds, "Under all providences maintain a contented heart with what the Lord allots you, be it more or less of the things of this world."[104] The believer must, therefore, keep an eye fixed heavenward through the course of this life. If not, he or she will be plagued by trouble and sorrow: "If we keep not our eye intently fixed upon the invisible and

---

100. Flavel, *Divine Conduct*, 4:429.
101. Flavel, *Divine Conduct*, 4:429.
102. See Flavel, *Divine Conduct*, 4:410, 480; *Caution to Seamen*, 5:334; and *Touchstone of Sincerity*, 5:618.
103. Flavel, *Divine Conduct*, 4:430.
104. Flavel, *Divine Conduct*, 4:431.

eternal things in the coming world, we shall feel ourselves fainting and dying away under the many troubles and afflictions of this world."[105]

The reason the Lord ordains suffering for His people in this life is so that they may "be quickened, and pricked forward with more haste to heaven...to look and long for the rest to come."[106] The believer journeys through this life "upon the road to the heavenly city." While this life is seen as "sharp and cold," Flavel explains, "heaven is warm and comfortable."[107] This longing for heaven is a reference to the believer's true affections and desires. The turning of one's treasure from this world to the next is, again, part of his or her sanctification and the increase of godliness. Suffering only shakes the foundation of one's hope in this world, while strengthening it for the next. Flavel offers this encouragement: "My name is blotted out of the earth, but still it is written in heaven. God hath taken my only son from me, but he hath given his only Son for me, and to me. He hath broken off my hopes and expectations as to this world, but my hopes of heaven are fixed sure and immoveable for ever. My house and heart are both in confusion and great disorder, but I have still an everlasting covenant, ordered in all things, and sure."[108]

To Produce a Sincere Faith, Devoid of Hypocrisy

The fifth reason that Flavel gives for God's ordaining suffering is to produce a sincere faith in the believer, devoid of hypocrisy. The added effect is that it can also distinguish the believer from the unbeliever. The effect is seen, therefore, in how one responds to suffering. God ordains suffering, then, to produce a real, sincere faith that separates the believer from the unbeliever.[109]

Flavel understands suffering to clear out the corruptions of the heart so as to leave it more faithful and sincere unto God. He writes,

---

105. Flavel, *Touchstone of Sincerity*, 5:576.
106. Flavel, *A Saint Indeed*, 5:448.
107. Flavel, *A Saint Indeed*, 5:461.
108. Flavel, *Balm of the Covenant*, 6:105.
109. Flavel calls hypocrites "Christ's summer friends." *Preparation for Sufferings*, 6:18.

"By these trials their sincerity is cleared.... One sharp trial wherein God helps us to be faithful, will do more to satisfy our fears, and resolve our doubts, than all the sermons that ever we heard in our lives could do."[110] In sufferings, "you have an opportunity to discover the sincerity of your love to God."[111] How can you discover your love to God? "When you can live upon him, and find enough in him, and constantly follow him, even when all external inducements and motives fail."[112] Suffering, then, becomes a way in which the believer can "discover" areas of insincerity and dishonesty in his or her relationship with God.

Flavel raises a point about the "advantages sincerity gives the soul for its establishment and perseverance in suffering times." He provides seven advantages. First, the sincerity produced dethrones idols of this world. Second, it "knits the soul to Christ, and union with him secures us in the greatest trials." Third, sincerity "sets the heart upon heaven, and things eternal." Fourth, it "drives but one design, and that is to please and enjoy God." Fifth, "sincerity brings a man's will into subjection to the will of God." Sixth, it "takes its measures of present things by the rules of faith and eternity." Seventh, sincerity alone hath all the heavenly aid and assistances to stability, and perseverance in suffering times."[113]

Suffering separates the believer from the unbeliever in the manner in which each responds to suffering. Flavel explains, "These sufferings and trials of the church, are ordained to free it of abundance of hypocrites, which were its reproach, as well as burden, Amos ix. 9, 10. Affliction is a furnace to separate the dross from the more pure and noble gold. Multitudes of hypocrites, like flies in a hot summer, are generated by the church's prosperity; but this winter weather kills them."[114] The unbeliever—who Flavel calls a "false professor"—experiencing suffering often "quits religion to save

---
110. Flavel, *Preparation for Sufferings*, 6:11.
111. Flavel, *A Saint Indeed*, 5:463.
112. Flavel, *A Saint Indeed*, 5:463.
113. Flavel, *Touchstone of Sincerity*, 5:577–78.
114. Flavel, *Preparation for Sufferings*, 6:11.

himself."[115] While suffering causes the elect to "cleave to [religion]," it causes the unbeliever to "forsake" it.[116] God ordains suffering to produce a greater sincerity of faith and to separate the Christian from the non-Christian. Flavel argues, "A wicked man finds his heart rising against God when he smites him; but a gracious heart cleaves the closer to him: he can love, as well as justify an afflicting God."[117]

We can see, therefore, that suffering—as it relates to exposing hypocrisy—comes as a sort of test or trial. It is not that God does not know who His people are, but that He provides testing so as to allow His people to know who they are. "Hypocrisy," Flavel writes, "cannot endure to come to the touchstone and test." Why? He answers: "For hypocrites, having a secret consciousness of their own guilt and unsoundness, know, that by this means their vain confidence would quickly be confuted, and all their reputation for religion blasted."[118] This Flavel sees as a blessing from God. "It is a great deal of honour put upon a poor worm, when God will every moment try him.... If God did not value you highly, he would not try you so frequently."[119] God ordains a trial or testing so as to reveal the Christian faith as the "greatest reality in the world."[120]

To Encourage Fellowship with God through Word, Prayer, and the Sacrament of the Lord's Supper

The sixth category that Flavel gives for why God ordains suffering is that suffering encourages greater fellowship with God through the Bible, prayer, and the Lord's Supper. It is clear that Flavel believes it is the Christian's duty to develop and cultivate a deeper and more meaningful relationship and fellowship with God—especially in

---

115. Flavel, *Touchstone of Sincerity*, 5:574.
116. Flavel, *Touchstone of Sincerity*, 5:577.
117. Flavel, *Divine Conduct*, 4:482.
118. Flavel, *Touchstone of Sincerity*, 5:588.
119. Flavel, *Touchstone of Sincerity*, 5:589–90. Similarly, he writes, "The design of Satan is to destroy you; but God's design is to try you." *Touchstone of Sincerity*, 5:575.
120. Flavel, *Touchstone of Sincerity*, 5:583.

times of suffering. Not only is the Christian to gain a greater knowledge of God and the Bible, he is to develop greater affection and love for God as well. Flavel writes, "Let there be no parting, sharing, or dividing of the affections betwixt God and the creature, let all the streams meet, and centre in thee only."[121] It is especially affliction that "drives them nearer to God, makes them see the necessity of the life of faith, with multitudes of other benefits."[122] Perhaps more clearly, Flavel explains:

> It is a good sign afflicting providences are sanctified to us, when we draw near to God under them, and *turn to him that smites us*.... But if God afflicts his own people with a sanctified rod, it awakens them to a more earnest seeking of God; it makes them pray more frequently, spiritually, and fervently than ever. When Paul was buffeted by Satan, he 'besought the Lord thrice,' 2 Cor. xii. 8. We may conclude our afflictions to be sanctified, and to come from the love of God to us when they do not alienate our hearts from God, but inflame our love to him.[123]

Flavel believed that suffering ushers the believer closer to God, with greater love and with greater fervor in communion with Him.[124] The opposite response is indicative of the unbeliever, though still possible for the believer. This is why Flavel writes to help guide his reader to respond to suffering rightly, without sin. This is also why

---

121. Flavel, *Token for Mourners*, 5:606. Similarly, he writes that calamities and afflictions "reduce our hearts from the creature to God, our only rest." *Divine Conduct*, 4:410; and, "Many a time providence hath spoken *instruction* in duty, *conviction* for iniquity, *encouragement* under despondency, but we regard it not. How greatly are we all wanting to our duty and comfort by this neglect! it would be but needful, therefore, to spread before you the loveliness and excellency of walking with God in a due and daily observation of his providences, that our souls may be fully engaged to it." *Divine Conduct*, 4:436.
122. Flavel, *Navigation Spiritualized*, 5:252.
123. Flavel, *Divine Conduct*, 4:482.
124. This "communing with God," according to Flavel, consists of two things: "God's manifestation of himself to the soul, and the soul's answerable returns to God. This is that, [*koinonia*], fellowship, we have here with God." *Divine Conduct*, 4:436.

he spends considerable ink on preparing for suffering.[125] Flavel does not desire his reader to necessarily seek a retreat from danger and suffering, but a prepared heart in danger and suffering.[126] As Flavel reminds his readers, "It is better for you to fall into any suffering, than into the least sin."[127]

Generally speaking, this "turning to God" in the midst of suffering, according to Flavel, includes (1) fellowship with God in His Word, the Bible; (2) fellowship with God through prayer; and (3) fellowship with God by partaking in the sacrament of the Lord's Supper.

Fellowship through the Word

Flavel held that all believers should study the Bible because it is the Christian's guide and directive: "Study the *word* more, and the concerns and the interests of the world less. The *word* is a light to your feet."[128] Flavel points his reader to "the scriptures, wherein are treasured up all the cordials and soul-reviving comforts."[129] Turning to the Bible, according to Flavel, should be both a preventative against sin as well as a balm to heal the wounds of sin. He explains, "Furnish your hearts richly with the word of God, which is their best preservation against sin. Keep the word, and the word will keep you."[130]

---

125. See, in particular, Flavel, *Preparation for Sufferings*, 6:3–82. In it he writes, "God hath fitted and prepared my heart for the greatest sufferings; this is the work of God." *Preparation for Sufferings*, 6:6. He adds later, "Readiness for sufferings will bring the heart of a Christian to an holy rest and tranquility, in a suffering hour, and prevent that anxiety, perturbation, and distraction of mind, which puts the sinking weight into afflictions." *Preparation for Sufferings*, 6:17. Flavel contends that there is "a twofold *preparation* or *readiness* for suffering; the one is *habitual*, the other *actual*." *Preparation for Sufferings*, 6:25. By habitual, he means the employment of various acts of obedience in looking ahead to the suffering time. By actual, he means the effects of those acts of obedience sealed to the believer.

126. Flavel, *Preparation for Sufferings*, 6:18. Such a preparation "prevents our own offence at sufferings." *Preparation for Sufferings*, 6:19.

127. Flavel, *Preparation for Sufferings*, 6:63.

128. Flavel, *Divine Conduct*, 4:470; cf. Ps. 119:105.

129. Flavel, *Tidings from Rome*, 4:580.

130. Flavel, *A Saint Indeed*, 5:504.

Turning to the Word—not just for knowledge and study, but for communing with God—is especially important during times of suffering. Flavel exhorts a mother grieving the loss of her son to "read frequently, ponder seriously, and apply believingly these scripture consolations and directions...and the God of all consolation be with you."[131] God applies His Word to the believer's soul in affliction so as to "sanctify" it. This is Flavel's view of what he called "sanctified afflictions." He explains, "We may call our afflictions sanctified, when *divine teachings* accompany them to our souls."[132] The promises made to the believer in God's Word may increase the faith of the sufferer during times of affliction. In this way, the Christian can come closer to God in fellowship. He writes, "Faith engages the presence of God, to be and abide with the soul in all its solitudes and sufferings: It lays hold upon the promises made to that purpose."[133] Thus we can see that Flavel believed the Scriptures should be applied to the sufferer for fellowship and for comfort: "[The Word] must be applied for our comfort in all inward and outward troubles."[134]

Fellowship through Prayer
As we have seen, affliction "awakens" the believer to "pray more frequently, spiritually, and fervently."[135] Flavel understood prayer[136] to be the "best way" for the Christian "to ease his heart when surcharged with sorrow."[137] He exhorts his reader to "follow every affliction with prayer, that God would follow it with his blessing."[138] Indeed, Flavel argues that it is this duty, in particular, that the sufferer should

---

131. Flavel, *Token for Mourners*, 5:607.
132. Flavel, *Divine Conduct*, 4:482.
133. Flavel, *Preparation for Sufferings*, 6:44.
134. Flavel, *Exposition of the Assembly's Catechism*, 6:274.
135. Flavel, *Divine Conduct*, 4:482.
136. Flavel, in line with the Westminster Shorter Catechism, defines prayer as "an offering up of our desires unto God, for things agreeable to his will, in the name of Christ, with confession of our sins, and thankful acknowledgment of his mercies." *Exposition of the Assembly's Catechism*, 6:291.
137. Flavel, *Preparation for Sufferings*, 6:64.
138. Flavel, *Method of Grace*, 2:390.

fulfill: "Doubtless [prayer] is of special use and service at all times to a Christian: But yet in suffering days it is of more than ordinary use and necessity, Heb. iv. 16. James v. 13. And therefore it is reckoned among those choice pieces of armour which suffering saints are to put on.... Many a saint, by prayer, hath sucked the breast of a promise, and then fell asleep by Divine contentment in the bosom of God."[139] Flavel regarded prayer to be not only an appropriate but also a necessary response of a believer undergoing suffering.[140] He follows a long line of Puritan thought on this point. Ralph Houlbrooke writes in his chapter "The Puritan Death-bed" that "the sick person's affliction comes from God, says Perkins. The right response to it is to seek reconciliation with God by means of fresh examination of heart and life, a confession to him of recent and serious sins, and renewed prayer."[141] Flavel, like William Perkins (1558-1602) and many others who followed, understood prayer to be a right response to affliction.[142]

Thus prayer is a central "duty" during times of suffering. It should be noted particularly that this duty is highlighted when suffering comes upon the believer. This is why Flavel argues, "By these troubles and distresses, [believers] are awakened to their duties, and taught to pray more frequently, spiritually, and fervently....

---

139. Flavel, *Preparation for Sufferings*, 6:64.

140. To shore up this study's thesis that Flavel not only believed in involuntaristic, passive responses, but also in voluntaristic, active responses—prayer is one clear example of a voluntaristic, active response. He writes, "I will...shew you that a Christian may improve himself to an excellent degree in it; and, lastly, prescribe some means for an improvement." He adds, "You must strive to excel in this, forasmuch as no grace within, or service without, can thrive without it." *Preparation for Sufferings*, 6:64–65.

141. Ralph Houlbrooke, "The Puritan Death-bed, c. 1560–c. 1660," in *The Culture of English Puritanism, 1560–1700*, ed. Christopher Durston and Jackqueline Eales (New York: Palgrave Macmillan, 1996), 125. Houlbrooke also notes, "Prayer—independent, varied, fervent, and often extemporary—occupies a prominent place in many accounts of Puritan death-beds." "Puritan Death-bed," 134.

142. Flavel writes, "The best posture we can wrestle with afflictions in, is to engage them upon our knees" as "Christ hastened to the garden to pray." *Fountain of Life*, 1:279.

I am sure the sweetest melody of prayer is upon the deep waters of affliction."[143] Flavel sees suffering that leads to a response of prayer as a "beneficial affliction."[144] He writes, "Blessed be God for the ordinance of prayer; how much are all the saints beholden to it, at all times, but especially in heart-sinking and distressful times?"[145]

Flavel's understanding of prayer as a means to greater fellowship with God during suffering includes the observation that the Bible provides directions, rules, and helps for prayer. He even says that "the whole word of God is of use to direct us in prayer."[146] In this way, the Christian may pray according to God's will and with morally (i.e., biblically) right petitions. The believer, therefore, should strive to align his or her mind and affections with God's as revealed in His Word, so that he or she may go to God in prayer rightly.[147] It is also clear that Flavel understood prayer, guided by the Word, to be activity superintended by the Holy Spirit, when he writes, "Now in our actual drawing near to God, the Spirit hath the chief and principal hand…. He suggests the matter of our prayers, and furnishes us with the materials."[148]

A final interesting element in Flavel's understanding of prayer as a right means to enter into greater fellowship with God in suffering is that he sees nothing wrong with complaining to God about afflictions experienced. "There is no sin in complaining to God," Flavel explains, "but much wickedness in complaining of him." He adds, "And happy were it if every afflicted soul would choose

---

143. Flavel, *Preparation for Sufferings*, 6:11.
144. Flavel, *Token for Mourners*, 5:650.
145. Flavel, *Token for Mourners*, 5:664.
146. Flavel, *Exposition of the Assembly's Catechism*, 6:294.
147. Flavel writes, "Hence we are informed, how necessary it is to acquaint ourselves with the mind of God, revealed in his word, that we may guide ourselves in prayer, both for matter and manner thereby: and not utter to God words without knowledge." *Exposition of the Assembly's Catechism*, 6:295.
148. Flavel, *Preparation for Sufferings*, 6:66. Similarly, he writes, "When *prayer*, the external, and the *Spirit*, the internal means are joined with them, then afflictions themselves become excellent means to promote salvation." *Divine Conduct*, 4:442.

this way to express his sorrows."[149] However, Flavel maintains, the Christian should not be presumptuous or arrogant in his complaining. "The afflicted Christian may, in an humble, submissive manner, plead with God, and be earnest for the removal of the affliction."[150] Therefore, prayer must be sincere, fervent, humble, and flowing from the heart of a regenerate person.[151] Prayer is a biblically right and active response to suffering that helps remove despair and sorrow from the believer.

Fellowship through the Lord's Supper
Finally, Flavel believed that God ordains suffering so as to encourage the believer in Christ to cultivate greater fellowship with Him through the sacrament of the Lord's Supper.[152] In *Preparation for Sufferings*, Flavel exhorts his reader to "improve well your sacrament seasons, those harvest days of faith: This ordinance hath a direct and peculiar tendency to the improvement and strengthening of faith."[153] It should be noted that Flavel held to Calvin's view of the "spiritual presence" of Christ in the Supper. In this way, there exists not only the external part, but also the "internal and heavenly, or spiritual" part. These internal parts of the Lord's Supper are "Christ's blood and Spirit." When a believer partakes of the Supper, "real exhibition of the blessings [are] signified and sealed."[154] As such, the elements of bread and wine in the sacrament both signify and seal the atonement of Christ, the promises of salvation, and the covenant of grace to the Christian who partakes of them by faith. Believers are to discover

---

149. Flavel, *Token for Mourners*, 5:614.
150. Flavel, *Token for Mourners*, 5:616. Flavel points to the example of Jesus: "Even our Lord Jesus Christ, in the day of his troubles, poured out his soul with strong cries and many tears."
151. Flavel, *Exposition of the Assembly's Catechism*, 6:292, 294.
152. He insists on writing of the Lord's Supper in particular (as opposed to baptism) because it is the continual sacrament of believers until the return of Christ, whereas baptism is to be administered but one time only.
153. Flavel, *Preparation for Sufferings*, 6:45.
154. Flavel, *Exposition of the Assembly's Catechism*, 6:278.

Christ in the sacrament and "to excite all their graces into vigorous acts for the applying of Christ to themselves."[155]

With this understanding of the Lord's Supper, it is easy to see how the sacrament can become a means whereby a believer may enjoy fellowship with God by partaking of it. In *Sacramental Meditations upon Divers Select Places of Scripture* (1679),[156] Flavel sets out to guide his reader in "drawing nigh to God" in the Lord's Supper, that he or she might find solace and comfort. He writes, "Now among all those ordinances, wherein the blessed God manifests himself to the children of men, none are found to set forth more of the joy of his presence, than that of the Lord's Supper: at that blessed table, are such sensible embraces betwixt Christ and believers, as do afford delight and solace, beyond the joy of the whole earth."[157] Flavel sees a direct relationship between the sufferings experienced by Christ—the benefits of which are represented and sealed in the Lord's Supper to the believer by faith—and the sufferings experienced by the Christian. He writes, "Should God spare the rod of affliction, it would not be for our advantage." With this in view, Flavel exhorts the believer to behold Christ in the Supper as a comparison to the sufferings he or she may experience ultimately: "All the wrath, all the curse, all the gall and wormwood was squeezed into Christ's cup, and not one drop left to imbitter ours."[158] Flavel summarizes this comparison rather succinctly when he writes, "Alas, there is no compare; there was more bitterness in one drop of his sufferings, than in a sea of

---

155. Flavel, *Exposition of the Assembly's Catechism*, 6:290.

156. The full title of this work is *Sacramental Meditations upon Divers Select Places of Scripture: Wherein Believers Are Assisted in Preparing Their Hearts, and Exciting Their Affections and Graces, When They Draw Nigh to God in That Most Awful and Solemn Ordinance of the Lord's Supper*. It was originally published as *Sacramental Meditations upon Divers Select Places of Scripture Wherein Believers Are Assisted in Preparing Their Hearts, and Exciting Their Affections and Graces, When They Draw Nigh to God in That Most Awful and Solemn Ordinance of the Lord's Supper*. (London: Printed for Jacob Sampson next door to the Wonder Tavern in Ludgate-street, 1679).

157. Flavel, *Sacramental Meditations*, 6:381.

158. Flavel, *Sacramental Meditations*, 6:425.

ours."[159] All comforts ultimately come from God through Christ; this is effectually presented in the Supper so that "whatever comfort, spiritual or natural, refreshes your souls or bodies, [it] is but a beam from that sun, a stream from that fountain."[160]

Flavel points to the Lord's Supper as being a "comforting" sacrament, calling it "the cup of consolation."[161] The Lord's Supper consoles the believer experiencing spiritual suffering by "healing the wounds which sin hath made in our consciences."[162] He correlates the close relationship of the external and internal sufferings whereby the "benefits of affliction" may come through fellowship with God in the Supper. In "The Seventh Meditation" in *Sacramental Meditations*, Flavel writes, "O how good it is for men to be brought into the straits of affliction." Speaking of a man with a sick child, he continues, "Had not this man fallen into this distress, it is not like that he had...arrived either to the sense of his grace, or the weakness of it."[163]

It should be clear by now that part of the active response of the Christian sufferer, according to Flavel, involved "drawing nigh to God" through the Word, prayer, and the sacrament of the Lord's Supper. These are reasons, too, for which God brings His people "into the straits of affliction."

To Bear Witness to the World

In the seventh reason for which God ordains suffering—to bear witness to a watching world—Flavel understands a twofold interrelated witness: (1) a witness to the reality of the gospel in the believer's life and its call to an unbelieving world to repent and believe in

---

159. Flavel, *Sacramental Meditations*, 6:440.
160. Flavel, *Sacramental Meditations*, 6:425.
161. Flavel, *A Familiar Conference between a Minister and a Doubting Christian, Concerning the Sacrament of the Lord's Supper*, 6:464. In this exchange, Flavel expresses the "doubting" Christian's position of being in a "deplorable condition," and therefore in need of taking the Supper. *Familiar Conference*, 6:462.
162. Flavel, *Familiar Conference*, 6:467.
163. Flavel, *Sacramental Meditations*, 6:427.

Christ for salvation; and (2) a witness of judgment upon those who remain impenitent.

First, God ordains suffering to bear witness to the reality of the believer's salvation in Christ to a watching world. Alexandra Walsham writes, "Every happening, catastrophic or trivial, was held to be relevant to the quest for assurance that one numbered among the 'saints,' a signpost concerning the Lord's soteriological intentions."[164] This idea can certainly be found in Flavel as well. Flavel writes, "The frequent trials of grace...prove beyond all words or argument that religion is no fancy, but the greatest reality in the world."[165] In a section titled "The Design of God in the Trial of His People,"[166] Flavel explains the correlation between the suffering of God's people and their witness in that suffering to the watching world: "But behold the wisdom and goodness of God exhibiting to the world the undeniable testimonies of the truth of religion, as often as the sincere professors thereof are brought to the test by afflictions from the hand of God."[167] One of the effects of this witness, Flavel points out, is that many "enemies of religion [are] brought over to embrace it, by the constancy and faithfulness of the saints in their trials and sufferings for it."[168] Flavel's desire is for his Christian reader to "convince the world of your constancy and cheerfulness in all your sufferings."[169]

Flavel's aim is also to encourage his reader to be faithful to God in the midst of suffering because this is one of God's reasons for ordaining it. This is why he exhorts his reader, "O beware what you do before the world...and as long as your carriage under trouble is so much like their own, they will never think your principles are better than theirs." He adds, "Wherefore hath God planted those excellent graces in your souls? but that he might be glorified, and you benefited, by the

---

164. Walsham, *Providence in Early Modern England*, 15.
165. Flavel, *Touchstone of Sincerity*, 5:583.
166. Flavel, *Touchstone of Sincerity*, 5:579–83.
167. Flavel, *Touchstone of Sincerity*, 5:583.
168. Flavel, *Touchstone of Sincerity*, 5:583.
169. Flavel, *Method of Grace*, 2:139.

exercises of them in tribulation."[170] Here, again, we see the dual aim of Flavel in his ministry to sufferers: the glory of God and their spiritual benefit. Drawing attention to God's glory, Flavel writes, "Hereby the most wise God doth illustrate the glory of his own name, clearing up the righteousness of his ways by the sufferings of his own people." The interesting thing about this sentence is that Flavel adds to it, "By this the wor[l]d shall see."[171] The saints' bearing witness to the reality of the gospel and the glory of God before a watching world, according to Flavel, is one of the reasons God ordains suffering.

The other important element here is that remaining faithful to God under suffering not only bears witness to the truth of the gospel but also pleases God. Flavel explains, "Unless you be diligent and successful in this work, though you should suffer; yet not like Christians; you will but disgrace religion, and the cause for which you suffer; for it is not simple suffering, but suffering as a Christian, that reflects credit on religion, and finds acceptation with God."[172] Bearing sin under suffering, Flavel contends, brings no honor to Christ. But bearing spiritual fruit under suffering brings Him glory.[173]

The second theme Flavel draws out from the first is that, while suffering bears witness to the reality of God's glory to the world, it also bears witness against those who remain in their unbelief. As those "frequent trials of grace" proved that the Christian faith is "the greatest reality in the world," so also do they "exhibit a full and living testimony against the atheism of the world."[174] By this, Flavel understands that judgment remains upon the unbeliever. Suffering that comes upon the believer is not only a testimony to his or her own salvation, but also a testimony to the absence of salvation in the unbeliever. Therefore,

---

170. Flavel, *Token for Mourners*, 5:648.
171. Flavel, *Preparation for Sufferings*, 6:9. It is clear that this is an error in the Banner of Truth reprint because Flavel continues in the same sentence, "...and by those very sufferings will provide for his own glory, which was by them clouded in the eyes of the world."
172. Flavel, *Preparation for Sufferings*, 6:53.
173. Flavel, *Preparation for Sufferings*, 6:53.
174. Flavel, *Touchstone of Sincerity*, 5:583.

Flavel has few words of comfort for individuals who remain in unbelief and sin: "I cannot offer [unbelievers] those reviving cordials that are contained in Christ and the covenant, for God's afflicted people."[175] God ordains suffering so that the believer may bear witness to the reality of salvation, God's own glory, and—as a necessary inference—the impending judgment of the unbelieving world.

To Cultivate Communion with Christ, the Greatest Sufferer

In Flavel's writings, the final major category for why God ordains suffering is so that the Christian sufferer may commune with Christ, the greatest sufferer, who travailed on his or her account. Not only does Christ know and understand the affliction of the elect, but the elect can—in a mystical sense—commune with Christ because He suffered for them.

The first element of this reason for God's ordaining suffering, according to Flavel, is that Christ "looks down from heaven upon all my afflictions, and understands them more fully than I that feel them."[176] This "understanding" is an important prerequisite for the believer's ability to enjoy communion with Christ in the midst of suffering. The necessary backdrop is an understanding that Jesus knows the suffering of His people. Flavel's follow-up comment here is worth noting: "In all your afflictions he is afflicted; tender sympathy cannot but flow from such intimate union."[177] Flavel understood the believer's union with Christ by faith as a foundation for his or her experiential communion with Christ. And one of the best expressions of this communion with Christ comes through the experience of suffering. God ordains suffering so that the believer ultimately might enjoy greater communion with Jesus, who has experienced suffering for believers.

The second element in this reason for God's ordaining suffering is so that the believer might see the exchange between Christ's

---

175. Flavel, *Token for Mourners*, 5:624.
176. Flavel, *Method of Grace*, 2:46. See also *Exposition of the Assembly's Catechism*, 6:193.
177. Flavel, *Method of Grace*, 2:46.

suffering and the believer's joy, even in the midst of the believer's experiential suffering. For example, Flavel writes of this exchange from God the Father's point of view:

> I will now manifest the fierceness of my heart to Christ, and the fulness of my love to believers. The pain shall be his, that the ease and rest may be theirs; the stripes his, and the healing balm issuing from them, theirs; the condemnation his, and the justification theirs; the reproach and shame his, and the honour and glory theirs; the curse his, and the blessing theirs; the death his, and the life theirs; the vinegar and gall his, the sweet of it theirs. He shall groan, and they shall triumph; he shall mourn, that they may rejoice; his heart shall be heavy for a time, that theirs may be light and glad for ever; he shall be forsaken, that they may never be forsaken; out of the worst of miseries to him, shall spring the sweetest mercies to them.[178]

We can see how this exchange provides the believer the positional and salvific benefits of Christ's atoning work but, as such, also provides the foundation from which the believer may share in Christ's sufferings when he or she experiences suffering. The Christian can know that Christ has experienced far greater suffering on his or her behalf. Therefore, "[Christ] hath fellowship with us in all our wants, sorrows, miseries and afflictions." Or to put it another way, "Our sufferings are his sufferings."[179] This last expression is Flavel's understanding of the apostle Paul's statement in Colossians 1:24, that Paul saw his sufferings as filling up that which was lacking in Christ's sufferings.[180] Noting his agreement with Augustine, Flavel understands from this text that Christ experiences sufferings in His mystical body—the church—after His ascension into heaven.[181]

---

178. Flavel, *Sacramental Meditations*, 6:426. See also *Method of Grace*, 2:151.
179. Flavel, *Method of Grace*, 2:151.
180. Flavel quotes this text, writing that Paul sought to "fill up that which was behind," the remainder of the "sufferings of Christ in his flesh." *Method of Grace*, 2:36.
181. Flavel, *Preparation for Sufferings*, 6:9.

Therefore, according to Flavel, Christ "still suffers in the sufferings of every saint."[182]

Union with Christ, then, becomes the foundation for communion with Christ in suffering: "Our union with Christ the Fountain of grace...is the true ground of our constancy and long suffering."[183] How should a Christian think of communion with Christ in suffering? Flavel's answer is twofold: "To take up our own cross, and follow Christ in a suffering path"[184] and to "apply the sufferings of Christ this day to thine own soul."[185]

An important element here is that when the believer sees and understands something of the suffering of Christ, he can then look at his own affliction and find no true comparison,[186] for "never had man such suffering to undergo as Christ."[187] The believer should look upon the afflicted Christ by faith and be thankful. Flavel expresses this spirit: "Alas! what are my sufferings compared with Christ's?"[188] Understanding and believing the severity of Christ's suffering then may result in a transformation in how the believer actually understands his or her own suffering. How does this happen? It happens by the bridge of faith between the promise and the experience. Flavel explains, "Faith entitles Christ to the believer's sufferings, and puts them upon his score; and so it exceedingly transforms and alters them."[189] Not only does faith alter the affliction experienced for the believer, it also "engages the presence of God, to be and abide

---

182. Flavel, *Method of Grace*, 2:36. Flavel warns, however, that this suffering of Christ in no way detracts from the complete suffering he experienced as Mediator; for those sufferings, Flavel writes, "are complete and full, and in that sense he suffers no more." For further explanation of Col. 1:24, see *Method of Grace*, 2:151, 222.

183. Flavel, *Preparation for Sufferings*, 6:30.
184. Flavel, *Preparation for Sufferings*, 6:3.
185. Flavel, *Sacramental Meditations*, 6:454.
186. Flavel, *Preparation for Sufferings*, 6:44.
187. Flavel, *Preparation for Sufferings*, 6:78.
188. Flavel, *A Saint Indeed*, 5:488.
189. Flavel, *Preparation for Sufferings*, 6:44.

with the soul in all its solitudes and sufferings: It lays hold upon the promises made to that purpose."[190]

This change in orientation of suffering comes by the Spirit, who gives that receiving faith, working in and through the believer. Thus, the Christian is able to see greater evidence of his or her status as a member of God's elect. Flavel assures his reader: "The more pleasure and delight you find in doing or suffering the will of God, the more of Christ's spirit is in you, and the more of his image is upon you."[191]

There is, as we have seen, a certain "sharing" in Christ's sufferings that establishes and cultivates greater communion with Christ experientially. Thus Flavel can pray, "O thou compassionate Samaritan! turn aside, and pour thy sovereign blood into these bleeding wounds."[192] Sharing in the sufferings of Christ, though, does not mean that the Christian is making atonement for sin, but that he or she experiences communion with Christ in his or her own sufferings. Thus we see in Flavel a reciprocal theme: when Christ is sharing in the believer's sufferings, the believer finds himself "drawing nigh" to Christ in His sufferings. This is why Flavel speaks of Christ's suffering with His people.[193]

In the final analysis, Flavel's twofold aim remains constant; namely, to promote the glory of God and the spiritual good of the elect. At the same time, Flavel maintains stern warnings of judgment—unsanctified afflictions—for the unbelieving world. While the sufferings that come upon the believer are meant for his or her ultimate good, the sufferings that come upon the unbeliever are signs and effects of God's wrath and impending judgment. The difference between the sanctified affliction and the unsanctified affliction is the effectual application of the substitutionary atonement of Christ. Therefore, as we have examined through the categories in this chapter, God ordains suffering to display His own glory, to benefit His people, and to execute justice upon the unbelieving world.

---

190. Flavel, *Preparation for Sufferings*, 6:44.
191. Flavel, *Sacramental Meditations*, 6:439.
192. Flavel, *Seaman's Catechism*, 5:341.
193. Flavel, *Fountain of Life*, 1:245.

CHAPTER FIVE

Flavel on the Right Response to Suffering

In *The Art of Suffering and the Impact of Seventeenth-Century Anti-Providential Thought*, Ann Thompson examines the nature of suffering in the seventeenth century and how the Puritans sought to alleviate the pain of sufferers through their writings by what she calls "the art of suffering." According to Thompson, while Puritans living in Stuart England certainly experienced great external suffering—"natural" disasters, death, persecution, or various socio-economic afflictions—their greatest sufferings were internal. It is important to remember that this finds agreement with Flavel and his understanding of the intensity of internal suffering.

Some of these internal effects include anguish, grief, distrust, discontentment, and impatience. Thompson explains, "It is these feelings rather than any external affliction, which constitute real suffering; and it is this kind of suffering, this inner distress caused by painful external circumstances, which is the target of the writer. Only if the inner distress is alleviated in some way will the external suffering be reduced to the level at which it can be borne."[1]

Thompson's book is critical to this study on Flavel's theology of suffering and sovereignty because she argues that the "art of suffering"—how a person responds to suffering—became a litmus test for demonstrating whether that individual was one of God's elect. During the later sixteenth and seventeenth centuries, an "anxiety-filled rift" existed between the objective knowledge of predestination and

---

1. Thompson, *Art of Suffering*, 3.

the subjective knowledge of one's assurance of being one of God's elect. The Puritans sought to demonstrate their status as members of God's elect by how they responded to affliction. If they responded with patience, thanksgiving, and an overall peace, for example, that gave evidence of their status as God's elect.[2]

Interestingly, Thompson sees a difference between the way in which the pre-1640s Puritan responded to suffering and the way in which the post-1640s Puritan responded to suffering. She explains, "In the sixteenth century the focus is on the cultivation of Christian patience, which is the condition we must fulfil if the affliction is to do its work."[3] This pre-1640s approach is what Thompson calls the "voluntaristic art of suffering," which goes beyond merely coping with affliction to trying to find ways in which to grow from affliction. By "voluntaristic," Thompson argues that the pressure came upon the Puritan sufferer to positively act in response to his or her suffering, and not just to "cope" with it, writing, "If the art of suffering up to the 1640s teaches the sufferer both how to 'cope with' and how to 'grow from' his affliction, the art of suffering in the second part of the seventeenth century teaches him only how to 'cope.'"[4] The accompanying goal of the Puritan writer was to defend God against those who would accuse Him either of not being perfectly good or of not being completely sovereign. In other words, the problem with evil and suffering is only a "problem" because the Puritans claimed that God is both good and all-powerful. The Puritans sought not only to give counsel to the sufferer in how rightly to respond to suffering, but also to defend both God's goodness and God's sovereignty.

Thompson argues that in pre-1640s England the Puritan was to "embrace the promises made in the Word" and, therefore, reap some spiritual benefits of affliction—from the text of Scripture to his or her real-time context of suffering.[5] In post-1640s England,

---

2. Thompson, *Art of Suffering*, 10–11.
3. Thompson, *Art of Suffering*, 11.
4. Thompson, *Art of Suffering*, 12.
5. Thompson, *Art of Suffering*, 85.

however, the art of suffering "is not divided into directions for the time before affliction comes and directions for the actual time of affliction."[6] Thompson explains, "It begins by defining an ideal state of mind (typically contentment, or silence, or resignation to the will of God); it includes a set of reasons which are designed to convince us of the necessity and utility of this state of mind; and it ends, almost always, with a set of directions on how to achieve it."[7] In other words, Thompson contends that the pre-1640s mindset sought spiritual benefit from suffering while the post-1640s mindset sought merely a contented state of mind. The pre-1640s thought was to see spiritual directions put into practice while the post-1640s thought was to simply listen and assent to the Puritan writer.[8]

Thompson's thesis raises several important questions as we examine Flavel's understanding of the right response to suffering. Does Thompson's claim find agreement with Flavel's theology? Did Flavel see the need to seek spiritual benefit from suffering, or was his aim simply to bring about contentment of mind in his reader?

According to Thompson, the main reason for this change in the response to suffering was that anti-providential thought began to increase as the seventeenth century progressed. The "doctrine of the profit of affliction" came under attack on a popular level toward the end of the seventeenth century.[9] Even still, the true providentialists referred to those who denied God's providence as "atheists," which was a highly pejorative term that encapsulated beliefs ranging from "gross immorality to the denial of the existence of God."[10]

In her final analysis, Thompson maintains that the pre-1640s way in which the Puritans responded to suffering "resolves the inherent contradictions between them and thus its internal coherence

---

6. Thompson, *Art of Suffering*, 85.
7. Thompson, *Art of Suffering*, 85–86.
8. Thompson, *Art of Suffering*, 88.
9. There came to be certain "popular" objections to providential thought, particularly, the seemingly inequitable distribution of good and ill or the inequitable treatment of the wicked and good. Thompson, *Art of Suffering*, 8–9.
10. Thompson, *Art of Suffering*, 7.

is sustained." However, the post-1640s art of suffering—of which Flavel was a member—"is incapable of resolving the inherent contradictions of its content and becomes internally incoherent and confused."[11] What are the reasons for her claim?

Thompson contends that the post-1640s Puritan writer's art of suffering does not allow his reader to "move out beyond the text to make a profitable use of his affliction because the line of the text leads him remorselessly back to the beginning of the text."[12] In other words, the reader is never independent of the Puritan writer's text, "never free to explore the depths of his own spirituality." While the pre-1640s reader was encouraged to make a profitable use of his or her affliction by moving out beyond the Puritan text, the post-1640s reader was bound to the time of the text and was given no imperative and no direction on how to make profitable and spiritual use of affliction. Furthermore, Thompson contends that "this radical transformation…suggests that the art of suffering in the second part of the seventeenth century is no longer informed with the belief that God intervenes in the world to direct specific suffering towards specific individuals."[13] Thompson, therefore, sees the post-1640s Puritan's "art of suffering"—including Flavel's—as lacking and internally incoherent because the writer is not free to find contentment, since he or she is not encouraged to pursue spiritual benefit or profitable use from his or her suffering. Did Flavel, living in the post-1640s world, believe that God does not intervene "in the world to direct specific suffering towards specific individuals"?

At least two questions significant to our study of Flavel's understanding of a right biblical response to suffering arise from Thompson's work:

---

11. Thompson, *Art of Suffering*, 18. The remainder of Thompson's book supports this basic thesis.
12. Thompson, *Art of Suffering*, 92.
13. Thompson, *Art of Suffering*, 92.

1. Did Flavel believe that one's status as a member of God's elect was experientially confirmed, at least in part, by how he or she responded to suffering?
2. Did Flavel believe that the right way to respond to suffering was to simply obtain a contented mindset—responding with passivity—or did he also contend that the believer should seek spiritual profit or benefit?

In the remainder of this chapter, we will argue that (1) Flavel did in fact see evidence of salvation in how one responded to suffering, and (2) Flavel not only argued for passive or "involuntaristic" responses to suffering, but also for active, "voluntaristic" responses as well.

Confirming Salvation by Christian Response

In Flavel's work *Preparation for Sufferings* he writes, "There is a great solemnity at the suffering and trial of a saint: heaven, earth, and hell, are spectators, observing the issue, and how the saints will acquit themselves in that hour."[14] How the Christian responds to suffering is of great concern for Flavel. The great cloud of witnesses observes the believer's response under affliction: "God, angels, and saints wait to see the glorious triumphs of their faith and courage, reflecting honour upon the name and cause of Christ" while "devils and wicked men gape for an advantage by their cowardice."[15]

It is essential to note that in many of his discourses on suffering Flavel primarily addresses fellow English Protestants. While he certainly has flares of polemical writing (i.e., against "Papists," Baptists, and Quakers), most of his *Works* may be classified as pastoral theology aimed at giving biblical counsel and instruction to fellow Protestant believers. Therefore, when he speaks of how "we" are to respond to suffering, he is addressing these fellow believers. This is obvious through the way in which he assumes saving faith in the reader, but, even more specifically, a Protestant—and to a lesser extent, a Reformed—faith. When he speaks boldly of justification, it seems as though he is more

---

14. Flavel, *Preparation for Sufferings*, 6:48.
15. Flavel, *Preparation for Sufferings*, 6:48.

affirming and confirming the already-held beliefs of his readers than trying to convince non-Reformed brethren.

There are places throughout each of Flavel's *Works*, however, in which he warns the reader against unbelief and the judgment of God upon the sin of unbelief. For example, he warns readers of "what a fearful thing it is to fall into the hands of a living God.... Wo to them that stand before God in their own persons, without Christ, how will justice handle them!"[16] These statements, however, seem to demonstrate a two-sided call of the gospel—both negative and positive. First, flee from sin so as to flee from the judgment to come. Second, run to Christ by faith and trust in Him as Savior and Lord.

In addition to this, Flavel warns against responding to suffering with "excessive sorrow" or "immoderate sorrow," especially when mourning the loss of a loved one. By these, Flavel argues that Christ "prohibits the excesses and extravagancies of our sorrow for the dead, that it should not be such a mourning for the dead as is found among the *heathen*, who sorrow without measure."[17] While some mourning is appropriate, "Christians ought to moderate their sorrows for their dead relations, how many afflicting circumstances, and aggravations soever meet together in their death."[18] When the believer faces suffering, he or she should respond directly to God about the circumstance. This response to God brings about a "happy soul." In this context, Flavel warns, "There is no sin in complaining to God, but much wickedness in complaining of him."[19]

Ann Thompson claims that the Puritans believed the way in which one responds to suffering validates his or her membership and status as God's elect, and this is consistent with Flavel's views. If "a tree is known by its fruit," the biblical response to suffering is the fruit of an elect man or woman. In fact, Flavel believed that only a true Christian has the ability to respond to suffering with faith, thanksgiving, and obedience to God. It is primarily by this reasoning

---

16. Flavel, *Sacramental Meditations*, 6:424.
17. Flavel, *Token for Mourners*, 5:610; cf. 5:608.
18. Flavel, *Token for Mourners*, 5:612.
19. Flavel, *Token for Mourners*, 5:614.

that Flavel held that a right response to suffering further validated one's sense of election. Furthermore, such a response also validated that individual's election to those in his or her community.[20]

Flavel, therefore, held to a consistent understanding of the moral ability of the elect to respond to suffering in a biblical way. The nonelect does not have the ability to respond to suffering with thanksgiving, joy, song, and submission.[21] Therefore, Flavel's exhortation is to the Christian. When Flavel speaks of the unbeliever and suffering, it is in terms of judgment, not blessing. That is why Flavel can write of Christians, "Afflictions and desertions seem to work against us, but being once put into the rank and order of causes, they work together with such blessed instruments, as word and prayer to an happy issue. And though the faces of these things that so agree and work together, look contrary ways; yet there are, as it were, secret chains and connexions of providence betwixt them, to unite them in their issue…. Cheer up then, O my soul, and lean upon this pillar of comfort in all distresses."[22]

For the unbeliever, suffering comes as judgment. For the believer, suffering comes as blessing even though he or she may not recognize it as such. Thus, Flavel seeks to strengthen his reader's faith in both God's sovereignty and God's goodness. Not only does this bring God glory, but it also brings the believer thanksgiving, joy, humility, and a host of other right responses to suffering.

The Passive Response: Submission to God's Will

According to Flavel, a God-glorifying response to suffering includes both passive and active elements. Specifically, the passive response includes a quiet and humble submission to God's will or the enduring of suffering with patience. Flavel writes, "Affliction is a pill, which being wrapt up in patience and quiet submission, may be easily swallowed."[23] This response—submission to God's will—is

---

20. See Flavel, *Touchstone of Sincerity*, 5:583.
21. The next chapter will examine the "active" or "profitable" way in which to respond to suffering.
22. Flavel, *Navigation Spiritualized*, 5:280.
23. Flavel, *A Saint Indeed*, 5:445.

a central exhortation that Flavel gives. Put simply, the believer is "to submit to the method Providence hath prescribed to us."[24] One way to do this, Flavel contends, is that the Christian should meditate upon God's attributes—especially His sovereignty, wisdom, and power. He explains: "Having taken a short view of this glorious chamber of God's power, absolutely in itself, and also in relation to his promises and providences, it remains now, that I press and persuade all the people of God under their fears and dangers, according to God's gracious invitation, to enter into it, shut their doors, and to behold with delight this glorious attribute working for them in all their exigencies and distresses."[25] Indeed, many of Flavel's writings on suffering guide the reader on how to respond to suffering with a God-centered, humble heart—in which God receives praise for His grace, wisdom, power, and sovereignty.

While an individual may not be able to control the circumstances of his or her external sufferings, Flavel argues the believer should respond to them with a quiet submission, patience, thanksgiving, and sustaining joy. He writes, "The cup of sufferings is a very bitter cup, and it is but needful that we provide somewhat to sweeten it, that we may be able to receive it with thanksgiving."[26] When faced with affliction, Christians are to "patiently bear the afflicting hand of God" so that they "are blessing, praising, and admiring God under their troubles."[27]

The Active Response: "Improving" Suffering for Profitable Use

While Flavel certainly believed that the suffering Christian should respond with a quiet submission and patience under the "afflicting

---

24. Flavel, *Balm of the Covenant*, 6:83.
25. Flavel, *Righteous Man's Refuge*, 3:351.
26. Flavel, *Preparation for Sufferings*, 6:4. One of the reasons for "thanksgiving" is that it is seen in light of hell. Flavel explains, "Though a *prison* looks sad and dismal, yet it is not *hell*: Oh bless God for that, that is a sad *prison* indeed.... If God exchange an *hell* for a *prison*, have you any cause to complain?" *Preparation for Sufferings*, 6:57.
27. Flavel, *Fountain of Life*, 1:368.

hand of God," he also believed that he or she should actively "improve" those afflictions for profitable use. In the first section, we examined Ann Thompson's claim that Puritans writing after the 1640s did not emphasize this active, voluntaristic response. However, it is clear that Flavel's desire was for the believer first to reflect upon these afflictive providences and then to act upon them by faith; or, as Flavel exhorts, to "improve them."[28] Specifically, Flavel points out, "Your concernment…is to improve the affliction to your own good."[29] Flavel believed that the improvement of suffering leads to greater faith in God and His promises: "Improve times of affliction for the increase of faith" so that "when difficult days come…we must get out our whole subsistence and livelihood by faith."[30]

Flavel's point here is visible in expressions like this: "How useful and beneficial are all your afflictions to you!"[31] Many times throughout his *Works*, Flavel mentions and argues for improving suffering for spiritual profit. Whether it is termed "improving grace,"[32] "beneficial afflictions,"[33] or the "improvement of faith,"[34] he clearly sought to encourage his reader to actively seek spiritual benefit in times of suffering. He writes, "To be free from affliction would be no benefit to believers, who receive so many benefits by it."[35] Such is Flavel's position on the art of suffering: "If afflictions be the way through which you must come to God, then never be discouraged at affliction; troubles and afflictions are of excellent use."[36]

In addition, it is "the duty of the people of God, to reflect upon these performances of providence for them at all times; but especially

---

28. Flavel, *Token for Mourners*, 5:649. These, then, become the believer's "profit." *Touchstone of Sincerity*, 5:579.
29. Flavel, *Token for Mourners*, 5:660.
30. Flavel, *Preparation for Sufferings*, 6:46.
31. Flavel, *Method of Grace*, 2:413.
32. Flavel, *Preparation for Sufferings*, 6:39–40. See also 6:45, 47.
33. Flavel, *Token for Mourners*, 5:650.
34. Flavel, *Preparation for Sufferings*, 6:41–42.
35. Flavel, *Method of Grace*, 2:272.
36. Flavel, *Method of Grace*, 2:286.

in times of straits and troubles."[37] This reflection, however, leads to action: "Without due observation of the work of providence, no praise can be rendered to God for any of them."[38] Moreover, "if these be forgotten, or not considered, the hands of faith hang down."[39] In whatever sufferings fall upon the elect, Flavel argues, they "are of great use to the people of God."[40] Reflecting upon God's providence in affliction should move one to action: "Many a time providence hath spoken *instruction* in duty, *conviction* for iniquity, *encouragement* under despondency, but we regard it not. How greatly are we all wanting to our duty and comfort by this neglect! it would be but needful, therefore, to spread before you the loveliness and excellency of walking with God in a due and daily observation of his providences, that our souls may be fully engaged to it."[41]

"Afflicting providences," as Flavel calls them, "are sanctified to us, when we draw near to God under them."[42] As God uses affliction to bring about His desired end in the lives of His people, Flavel cautions his reader to "not be too hasty to get off the yoke which God hath put upon your neck." He adds, "O desire not to be delivered from your sorrows one moment before God's time for your deliverance be fully come also."[43] Flavel does not want his reader necessarily to seek a retreat from suffering, but a prepared heart in suffering.[44] Flavel's hope is that when the hour of affliction comes the believer will act rightly, according to the commands and principles set forth in the Bible.

As we have seen, Flavel sought to alleviate the internal and spiritual pain of his reader by applying biblical indicatives as well as biblical imperatives. Not only did he want his reader to find

---

37. Flavel, *Divine Conduct*, 4:413.
38. Flavel, *Divine Conduct*, 4:414.
39. Flavel, *Divine Conduct*, 4:415.
40. Flavel, *Divine Conduct*, 4:487.
41. Flavel, *Divine Conduct*, 4:436.
42. Flavel, *Divine Conduct*, 4:482.
43. Flavel, *Token for Mourners*, 5:605.
44. This theme encompasses Flavel's entire *Preparation for Sufferings*, 6:3–83.

contentment of mind through a humble submission to God's will, but he also provided directives on how to appropriately respond to suffering for profitable use.

The last chapter examined many of these active responses by acknowledging the purposes for which God ordains suffering. For example, when affliction strikes, the believer is to reflect on how that suffering might reveal something of his own sin, warn him of greater sin, and actually mortify that sin. Or, to take another example, if persecution strikes a believer's household, he may actively pursue greater fellowship and communion with God in the Word, in prayer, or in the sacrament of the Lord's Supper. Therefore, the reasons God ordains suffering are the right responses that believers should exhibit. The purpose of God and the response of man meet for His glory and the believer's joy.

CHAPTER SIX

The Assurance of Salvation in Flavel's Ministry to Sufferers

According to Flavel, cultivating greater assurance of salvation is an important way to experience comfort and hope in the midst of suffering. Throughout his *Works*, Flavel points his readers to various reasons they should be assured of their citizenship in God's kingdom and the status of being God's adopted children. As an heir of the Westminster Assembly, Flavel leaned heavily upon its documents and put pastoral flesh on the bones of its teaching. This chapter seeks to examine Flavel's development of Westminster's doctrine of assurance, generally, and how he sought to provide pastoral guidance and ministry to those who were suffering, in particular.

The Post-Westminster "Quest" for Assurance: Flavel and His Ministry to Sufferers

In "The Logic of Assurance in English Puritan Theology," R. M. Hawkes writes, "In English Puritan theology, the doctrine of assurance is of abiding importance. Any description of the aims of Puritanism must include the twin objectives of reforming the hearts of men along with the reform of external structures. As the external reform of the church consisted of a thorough restructuring according to the blueprint of Scripture, so the internal reformation of the Puritan's pilgrim soul was to seek an assured faith following God's revealed way to himself."[1] Seeking this assured faith was certainly true

---

1. R. M. Hawkes, "The Logic of Assurance in English Puritan Theology," *Westminster Theological Journal* 52 (1990): 248.

in Flavel's theology, as we shall see, but this "quest" for assurance was a common theme of post-Westminster Puritan theology as a whole.[2]

Additionally, many of the post-Westminster Puritans incorporated the doctrine of assurance into their ministry to sufferers. For example, Thomas Watson (c. 1620–1686), in a sermon series on the Westminster Shorter Catechism titled *A Body of Practical Divinity* (1692),[3] writes of the effect of having assurance in times of suffering, "Assurance would bear up the heart in sufferings, it would make a Christian endure troubles with patience and cheerfulness.... Assurance gives the light of comfort in affliction. Heb. x. 34., Ye 'took joyfully the spoiling of your goods, knowing in yourselves,' &c. there was assurance. He that hath assurance can rejoice in tribulation; he can gather grapes of thorns, and honey out of the lion's carcase."[4] Very pointedly, Watson argues that it is precisely assurance that bears up the heart in sufferings. When a Christian finds himself in the thick of affliction, assurance becomes his "light of comfort."

Similarly, John Owen (1616–1683) in his post-Westminster work *A Discourse Concerning the Holy Spirit* (1674), writes that God "hath designed the generality of his elect to a poor, low, and afflicted condition in this world." Yet, "it hath the same *tendency* and effect in the *assurance* we have from thence, that notwithstanding all

---

2. For an in-depth study of the doctrine of assurance before the Westminster Assembly, see Joel R. Beeke, "Assurance Prior to the Westminster Assembly," in *The Quest for Full Assurance: The Legacy of Calvin and His Successors* (Edinburgh: Banner of Truth, 1999), 7–108. The pre-Westminster understanding of assurance as well as the Westminster Assembly's development of assurance finds roots in the theology of William Perkins (1558–1602). See Jacqueline Eales, "A Road to Revolution: The Continuity of Puritanism, 1559–1642," in *Culture of English Puritanism*, ed. Durston and Eales, 197.

3. First published after Watson's death in 1692 (ironically, the same year as Flavel's *Exposition of the Assembly's Catechism* was published), *A Body of Practical Divinity* became Watson's most famous work. It contains 176 sermons, in expositional style, on the Westminster Shorter Catechism.

4. Thomas Watson, *A Body of Practical Divinity, In a Series of Sermons on the Westminster Shorter Catechism* (Aberdeen: George King, 1838), 230.

the oppositions we meet withal, we shall not utterly and finally miscarry."[5] Owen's point is that, despite the afflictions of this present life, the believer should look unto God's promises in the final perseverance of the elect as grounds for assurance.

John Bunyan (1628–1688) writes in *Seasonable Counsel; Or, Advice to Sufferers* (1684),[6] of the assurance that his reader should have in times of affliction; particularly of affliction being a sign of sonship. He explains, "Chastisements are a sign of sonship, a token of love."[7] Moreover, he writes, "There can be no sorrow, affliction, or misery invented, by which the devil may so strongly prevail, as thereby to pluck the soul out of the hand of him who has received it, to keep it from falling, and perishing thereby."[8] Bunyan sought to minister to his suffering reader by pointing him to the assurance of his eternal salvation—despite his experience of "sorrow, affliction, or misery."

Thus we see that many post-Westminster Puritans found a balm for suffering in the doctrine of Christian assurance. Flavel was no exception. He took Westminster's theology of assurance and clothed it with pastoral ministry for sufferers. But what exactly did the Westminster Assembly offer in its explication of assurance? Moreover, how and by what other doctrines was the doctrine of Christian assurance built up and supported?

In his book *The Quest for Full Assurance*, Joel Beeke examines the doctrine of assurance in the Westminster Confession of Faith, especially chapter 18.1, "Of Assurance of Grace and Salvation," which states that those who "truly believe in the Lord Jesus…

---

5. John Owen, Pneumatologia, *or, A Discourse Concerning the Holy Spirit*, in *The Works of John Owen* (1850–1853; repr., Edinburgh: Banner of Truth, 1965), 3:601.

6. First published in London for Benjamin Alsop at the Angel and Bible in the Poultry, 1684.

7. John Bunyan, *Seasonable Counsel; Or, Advice to Sufferers*, in *The Works of John Bunyan*, ed. George Offor (1854; repr., Edinburgh: Banner of Truth, 1991), 2:694–95.

8. Bunyan, *Seasonable Counsel*, 2:699.

may, in this life, be certainly assured that they are in the state of grace."[9] Because Flavel was an heir of the standards of the Westminster Assembly, his *Exposition of the Assembly's Shorter Catechism* is an important element for understanding his doctrine of assurance. The *Exposition* is therefore an integral part of how Flavel pastorally developed Westminster's teaching on assurance.[10] What are the important elements of the Westminster Confession's teaching on assurance? Beeke codifies four distinct elements:[11]

1. It teaches that saving faith must be distinguished from assurance.[12] Assurance grows out of saving faith, but it is not the essence of faith. This division has at least two pastoral and ministerial implications: (1) a Christian may doubt his or her faith even though he or she has the seed of saving faith, and (2) a Christian can find comfort in suffering, knowing that, although his or her assurance waxes and wanes due to sin, he or she still has saving faith.

2. It teaches that a Christian comes to experience assurance through the work of the Holy Spirit—whether it be by the Spirit's application of God's promises in Christ or through the Spirit's witness by the Word that Christ is his or her personal Savior.[13]

---

9. A similar idea is explained in Walsham, *Providence in Early Modern England*, 15.

10. As mentioned previously, this work was published posthumously as *An Exposition of the Assemblies Catechism, with Practical Inferences from Each Question: As It Was Carried on in the Lords Days Exercises in Dartmouth, in the First Year of Liberty, 1688* (London: Printed for Tho. Cockerill, at the Three Legs in the Poultry over against Stocks-Market, 1692).

11. Beeke also categorizes these four parts in his related article "Personal Assurance of Faith: The Puritans and Chapter 18.2 of the Westminster Confession," *Westminster Theological Journal* 55 (1993): 3. Moreover, these four parts correspond to themes in the four sections in chapter 18 of the Westminster Confession of Faith, respectively.

12. Beeke, *Quest for Full Assurance*, 113.

13. Beeke, *Quest for Full Assurance*, 115.

3. It teaches that the assurance wrought by the Holy Spirit is based upon the covenant of grace and the salvation secured by Christ, which in turn is grounded upon decretal election. God's covenant cannot be broken because it is fixed by God's eternal and sovereign decree.[14]

4. Assurance, though incomplete in this life due to sin, must be sought after through the means of grace—in particular, Word, prayer, and sacrament.[15]

Are these elements true in Flavel's theology of assurance? If so, how do they relate to his ministry to those who are suffering? This study contends that Flavel did, in fact, believe these principles as taught in the Westminster Confession of Faith and will explore how these principles laid the theological foundation from which Flavel was able to provide assurance and hope in his pastoral ministry to the suffering believer.

Assurance, Comfort, and Faith in Flavel's Ministry to Sufferers

Flavel believed that "there is nothing in this world, which true Christians more earnestly desire, than to be well assured and satisfied of the love of Jesus Christ to their souls."[16] The Christian who possesses assurance says, "I believe and am sure that Christ died for me, and that I shall be saved through him."[17] Flavel also

---

14. Beeke, *Quest for Full Assurance*, 116.

15. Beeke, *Quest for Full Assurance*, 118, 152.

16. Flavel, *Sacramental Meditations*, 6:451. See also *Righteous Man's Refuge*, 3:380. Flavel writes, "The scripture tells us of an assurance of understanding, hope, and faith. All these graces are precious in themselves but the assurance of each of them is the most sweet and pleasant part." *Sacramental Meditations*, 6:452.

17. Flavel, *Method of Grace*, 2:115. Flavel writes, "Let none conclude, that seeing there are so many mistakes committed…that therefore assurance must needs be impossible, as the Papists affirm it to be." *Method of Grace*, 2:363. Elsewhere, he explains, "[Papists] deny the possibility of the assurance of salvation in this life." *Tidings from Rome*, 4:580. Flavel sees this impossibility of assurance for Roman Catholics in their doctrine: "That assurance is one of the

believed that experiential assurance comes as an outworking of a right understanding of suffering. Knowing and believing the various reasons God ordains suffering leads to a strengthening of faith and thus to a greater assurance of one's salvation. Flavel writes pointedly, "Trials are the high way to assurance."[18] God will test and try the believer "by prosperity and by adversity, by persecutions and temptations, and he shall see his heart is better than he suspects it to be. This shall be the day of resolution to his fears and doubts."[19] Interestingly, Flavel sees the "usual season of assurance" to be "the time of greatest sufferings for Christ."[20] As trials and afflictions provide the platform for assurance, so also they provide the platform for comfort.

The relationship between assurance and comfort is vital to understanding Flavel's ministry to the suffering believer. Flavel sees two sorts of comfort, "natural" and "spiritual."[21] While there are certain times when the Christian is right to experience natural comfort, "there is no season wherein spiritual joy and comfort in God is unseasonable." He adds, "This spiritual joy or comfort is nothing else but the cheerfulness of our heart in God, and the sense of our interest in him, and in his promises."[22] Having this "spiritual joy or comfort," no doubt involves having saving faith in God and His promises. However, Flavel contends that *"Faith may be separated from comfort, but assurance cannot."*[23] This is why Flavel writes that "a man may be saved, and in Christ, without [assurance]."[24]

---

great difficulties in religion, is a great truth; but that it is therefore unattainable in this world, is very false. Popish doctrine indeed makes it impossible." *Touchstone of Sincerity*, 5:525.
    18. Flavel, *Touchstone of Sincerity*, 5:581.
    19. Flavel, *Touchstone of Sincerity*, 5:581.
    20. Flavel, *Exposition of the Assembly's Catechism*, 6:201.
    21. Flavel, *Divine Conduct*, 4:428.
    22. Flavel, *Divine Conduct*, 4:428–29.
    23. Flavel, *Divine Conduct*, 4:429.
    24. Flavel, *Exposition of the Assembly's Catechism*, 6:201.

Faith can be separated from comfort because the latter is but a fruit of the former.[25] On the other hand, Flavel believed that if a Christian has assurance, he will necessarily also have comfort. This is why comfort and assurance go hand in hand. The difference between assurance and comfort is in the order experienced: assurance leads to comfort, not the reverse. Where Flavel seeks to confirm the believer's assurance of salvation, he also seeks to provide his reader with greater comfort. On the other hand, it is wrong to place "the essence of faith...in full assurance."[26] Therefore, we see a division between faith and assurance, but a necessary connection between assurance and comfort.

Flavel writes in his *Exposition of the Assembly's Shorter Catechism*, "Faith in Jesus Christ is a saving grace, whereby we receive and rest upon him alone for salvation, as he is offered to us in the gospel."[27] In response to this definition, Flavel asks, "Is true faith exclusive of all fears and doubts?" His answer: "No; it is not, but true believers are troubled with many fears and doubtings."[28] Therefore, true faith can lack assurance. The foundation of saving faith, Flavel explains, lies in the power of God and the truth and faithfulness of God's promises.[29]

Flavel's desire was to provide comfort to afflicted saints by demonstrating theological and practical grounds of their assurance of salvation.[30] Faith unites the believer to Christ so that the believer's sin is imputed to Christ and Christ's righteousness is imputed to the believer. Upon this "exchange," the believer is declared "not

---

25. Flavel also notes that joy and peace are outworkings of assurance. *Exposition of the Assembly's Catechism*, 6:201–2. See also *Antipharmacum Saluberrimum*, 4:553.
26. Flavel, *Method of Grace*, 2:123.
27. Flavel, *Exposition of the Assembly's Catechism*, 6:262.
28. Flavel, *Exposition of the Assembly's Catechism*, 6:263.
29. Flavel, *Exposition of the Assembly's Catechism*, 6:264.
30. This is evident in Flavel's section titled "Containing the last use of the point, by way of support and comfort to poor trembling souls, who do take pains to make themselves ready for sufferings," in *Preparation for Sufferings*, 6:79–83.

guilty" or "righteous" before God. This is the doctrine of justification.³¹ This point is important because Flavel calls assurance "the fruit of justification."³²

As an outworking or "fruit" of justification, assurance is not only possible to be attained in this life, but also "all Christians are commanded to strive for it."³³ However, only one type of assurance can be perfected in this life. Flavel seems to equate saving faith with "objective assurance," which he sees as a seal that God has indeed saved His elect. Flavel separates this objective assurance from "subjective or personal assurance"—the belief that Christ did in fact die for me. While objective assurance is unwavering and sure, subjective assurance "admits doubts and fears" and therefore is not perfect until glorification in heaven.³⁴ The notion of partaking in the "joys of heaven" in this life is experienced through assurance. He exhorts, "You that have received Jesus Christ truly, give yourselves no rest till you are fully satisfied that you have done so; acceptance brings you to heaven hereafter, but assurance will bring heaven into your souls now. O, what a life of delight and pleasure doth the assured believer live!"³⁵ Flavel understands that one inference from the doctrine of assurance is that "all the joys of heaven are not to come; but some [are] communicated in this life."³⁶

---

31. For Flavel's understanding of justification, see his *Exposition of the Assembly's Catechism*, 6:196–97. There he writes that the two parts of justification are "the pardon of sin" and "the acceptation of our persons as righteous." Furthermore, he explains that this application comes "by faith," not works.

32. Flavel, *Exposition of the Assembly's Catechism*, 6:200.

33. Flavel, *Exposition of the Assembly's Catechism*, 6:200. See also *Righteous Man's Refuge*, 3:395.

34. Flavel, *Exposition of the Assembly's Catechism*, 6:200. Similarly, he writes, "Assurance is as much too high, being found only in some eminent believers: and in them too but at some times. There is many a true believer to whom the joy and comfort of assurance is denied.... A man must be a believer before he know himself to be so." *Method of Grace*, 2:114.

35. Flavel, *Method of Grace*, 2:138.

36. Flavel, *Exposition of the Assembly's Catechism*, 201.

Assurance is built up and strengthened for the Christian—especially for the suffering Christian—through the work of the Holy Spirit, who increases a greater understanding and faith in the believer's decretal election, in his status as a member of God's covenant of grace, in his union with Christ, and through the various "means of grace" God has appointed to establish assurance. Flavel maintains, "Assurance is a lump of sugar, indeed, in the bitter cup of death; nothing sweetens like it."[37] Similarly, he writes, "Assurance will call a bloody death a safe passage to Canaan through the Red sea."[38] Elsewhere, he writes of the importance of assurance in suffering:

> In a word [assurance] is a sweet support, in all the troubles and afflictions on this side the grave. Let the assured soul be cast into what condition the Lord pleases; be it upon a bed of sickness; yet this gives his soul such support and comfort, that he shall not say, I am sick. Sin being forgiven, the soul is well, when the body is in pain, Isa. xxiii. 24. Let him be cast into a prison, here is that which will turn a prison into a paradise, Acts v. 41. Let him be pinched with outward want; this will supply all.[39]

The remainder of this chapter will examine how Flavel utilized each of these particular doctrines as grounds of assurance in his ministry to sufferers. Furthermore, it will be shown that Flavel's thought and ministry find agreement with the principles of assurance laid out by the Westminster Assembly.

The Holy Spirit in the Work of Assurance

Summarizing the Puritan understanding of the role of the Holy Spirit in the doctrine of assurance, Beeke writes, "At every point in true assurance, the activity of the Spirit is essential. Without the application of the Spirit, the promises of God lead to self-deceit and fruitless lives."[40] In line with the Westminster Shorter Catechism,

---

37. Flavel, *Treatise of the Soul of Man*, 3:11.
38. Flavel, *Practical Treatise of Fear*, 3:304.
39. Flavel, *Sacramental Meditations*, 6:453.
40. Beeke, "Personal Assurance of Faith," 28.

Flavel teaches that the Holy Spirit applies the redemption purchased by Christ to the elect. How does he do this? "By working faith in us, and thereby uniting us to Christ in our effectual calling."[41] The effect of the Spirit's work, then, is to unite the believer to Christ. This union is never to be dissolved, even in the face of tribulation, persecution, famine, nakedness, peril, or sword.[42] As such, the souls of those effectually called are never lost, but are kept safe by God for eternity.

Flavel raises the question: "On what testimony is personal assurance built?" Answer: "Upon the testimony of God's Spirit witnessing with ours." As noted earlier, he writes that the most "usual season of assurance" is "the time of greatest sufferings for Christ."[43] In other words, assurance shines brightest during suffering because, when faced with the loss of that which is of this world, the believer may rest in the knowledge that he or she will gain that which is in the world to come. This is why Flavel argues that the believer may have "joy unspeakable amidst outward troubles."[44]

How does a believer attain assurance? While he or she may strive by the various means of God's appointment, Flavel maintains, it is the Holy Spirit that imparts various measures of assurance to the believer. He explains, "O when a man considers, that the whole weight of his eternal happiness or misery, depends upon the resolution of these questions, Am I in Christ; or am I not! it will make him tremble to determine. There be many holy, humble, diligent, and longing souls, to whom it is denied: it is arbitrarily dispensed by the pleasure of the Spirit, to whom he will: and such favors are rare, even among true believers."[45] It is important to note, however, that while the Spirit is the one who effects this assurance in the Christian's life, the Christian is to carefully keep his or her own heart desiring God and the things of God. Therefore, Flavel warns his reader not to neglect those means by which the Spirit increases assurance in

---

41. Flavel, *Exposition of the Assembly's Catechism*, 6:191.
42. Flavel, *Exposition of the Assembly's Catechism*, 6:192.
43. Flavel, *Exposition of the Assembly's Catechism*, 6:201.
44. Flavel, *Exposition of the Assembly's Catechism*, 6:201.
45. Flavel, *Sacramental Meditations*, 6:453.

the believer's life. He writes, "God doth not usually indulge lazy and negligent souls with the comforts of assurance; he will not so much as seem to patronize sloth and carelessness."[46]

The Spirit's Sealing Work

How does the Spirit work assurance into the conscience of the believer? By "sealing" the believer's faith and interest in Christ.[47] Flavel's understanding of the sealing work of the Holy Spirit, its effect of assurance, and its pastoral consolation to the suffering Christian is crucial. First, it is important to grasp that Flavel held to a twofold sealing. He explains, "There is a twofold sealing, and a twofold comfort: The Spirit sealeth both objectively, in the work of sanctification; and formally, in giving clear evidence of that work. Thou mayest be sealed in the first, whilst thou are not yet sealed in the second sense: If so, thy condition is safe, although it be at present uncomfortable."[48] The comforts—both actual and in the outworking of the actual—point back to the twofold sealing as their foundation. In other words, true comfort (no matter the circumstances) is found as an effect of the Spirit's sealing work of assurance.

Flavel understands the Holy Spirit to be the one who effects subjective or "formal" assurance: "The Author of assurance, which is

---

46. Flavel, *A Saint Indeed*, 5:434–35. In the same section, he adds, "The improvement of our graces depends upon the keeping [of] our hearts; I never knew grace thrive in a negligent and careless soul." Likewise, he writes, "Would we pray more, and strive more, would we keep our hearts with a stricter watch, mortify sin more thoroughly, and walk before God more accurately; how soon may we attain this blessed assurance, and in it an excellent cure for our distracting and slavish fears." *Practical Treatise of Fear*, 3:304.

47. In contrast to this subjective sealing and assurance, Flavel notes that there is an "objective seal" in which the Spirit "sanctifies us really by the infusion of grace" and "seals us by way of distinction from other men." *Sacramental Meditations*, 6:404. Elsewhere, he writes that the Spirit works in believers "objectively, i. e. by working those graces in our souls which are the conditions of the promise, and so the Sprit and his graces in us, are all one." *A Saint Indeed*, 5:434. See also *Treatise of the Soul of Man*, 2:575.

48. Flavel, *Method of Grace*, 2:343.

the Spirit, he is the keeper of the great seal of heaven; and it is his office to confirm and seal the believer's right and interest in Christ and heaven." He does this "by opening and applying the promises to believers."[49] More specifically, Flavel adds, "The sealing of the Spirit is, his giving a sure and certain testimony to the reality of that work of grace he hath wrought in our souls, and to our interest in Christ and the promises, thereby satisfying our fears and doubts about our estate and condition."[50]

Here it can be seen that Flavel held to a close relationship between the sealing of the Spirit and the consolation brought to the believer by having a greater certainty of his or her election and salvation, which is given to the believer by way of God's promised sealing by the Spirit: "Though God hath reserved to himself a liberty of afflicting his people, yet he hath tied up his own hands by promise never to take away his loving-kindness from them."[51] The Spirit makes use of the combination of the grace already implanted within the soul and the promises of God written in the Scriptures to bring about rest, comfort, and peace—even in the midst of great suffering.[52]

The fact that believers "are sealed upon some imminent hazard they have been exposed to for Christ, or some extraordinary sufferings they have undergone for Christ" is, for Flavel, an important element in his ministry to sufferers.[53] By showing his sufferers that they very well may be sealed by the Spirit in the midst of suffering, he intends to minister to them and to bring them greater comfort and hope. Flavel writes, "Thus the martyrs were many times sealed in the depth of their sufferings." His point to a suffering—or would-be suffering—reader is that even "dying-times prove [to be]

---

49. Flavel, *Sacramental Meditations*, 6:402.
50. Flavel, *Sacramental Meditations*, 6:402.
51. Flavel, *A Saint Indeed*, 5:441.
52. Flavel, *Sacramental Meditations*, 6:403. He adds, "The Spirit helps us to reflect upon what hath been done by him formerly upon our hearts." *Sacramental Meditations*, 6:404.
53. Flavel, *Sacramental Meditations*, 6:405.

sealing-times to many souls."⁵⁴ Moreover, "the assured Christian looks upon his death as his wedding-day."⁵⁵ By showing this, Flavel seeks to bring consolation to the sufferer by imparting the knowledge of the Spirit's work of assurance so that he or she might know that the Spirit "enableth believers to glory in tribulation."⁵⁶

The Holy Spirit and Adoption

Attaining and retaining certain knowledge is a key theme in Flavel's understanding of assurance. He writes, "Hereby we know that he abideth in us, by the Spirit which he hath given us."[57] While this knowledge leading to greater assurance certainly rests in the believer's knowledge of his union with Christ,[58] it is particularly seen in the doctrine of adoption. Adoption stands out not only as a way in which the Spirit attests to the Christian's assurance, but also pastorally as a primary relief to the suffering Christian, bringing comfort and consolation.

Flavel sees adoption as a "practical syllogism": "All that truly have received Christ Jesus, they are the children of God. I have truly received Jesus Christ. Therefore I am the child of God."[59] Truly receiving Christ, however, does not necessarily mean that the believer will have great faith. Even weak faith truly receives Christ as Savior, which adds the bonus of becoming an adopted son or daughter of God. Flavel beautifully elaborates, "O believer, though the arms of thy faith be small and weak, yet they embrace a great Christ, and receive the richest gift that ever God bestowed the world: no sooner art thou

---

54. Flavel, *Sacramental Meditations*, 6:405. Interestingly, Flavel sees that death can actually be an object of desire when put in the light of assurance: "If once the great question of our interest in Christ be thoroughly decided, and all be clear betwixt us and our God, we shall find life a matter of patience, and death the object of desire." *Sacramental Meditations*, 6:408.
55. Flavel, *Practical Treatise of Fear*, 3:304.
56. Flavel, *Treatise of the Soul of Man*, 2:576.
57. Flavel, *Method of Grace*, 2:328.
58. Flavel, *Method of Grace*, 2:329. See the following section "Union with Christ as Ground for Assurance."
59. Flavel, *Method of Grace*, 2:123.

become a believer, but Christ is in thee the hope of glory; and thou hast authority to become a son or daughter of God; thou hast the broad seal of heaven to confirm thy title and claim to the privileges of adoption."[60] Flavel sees the doctrine of adoption as a key ministry tool to bring comfort to his reader because it assures him or her of saving grace. Furthermore, the Holy Spirit attests to the believer's adoption. "The Spirit, indeed, assures by witnessing our adoption."[61]

The Spirit "first infuses the grace, and then opens the eye of the soul to see it."[62] The comfort of adoption brings joy in the midst of suffering and affliction. The Spirit does this work of assurance through various means by which the believer is to act in faith. Flavel laments, however, at how often believers fail to act in faith: "What a poor house is kept by many of God's own children; living between hopes and fears, seldom tasting the riches and pleasures, the joys and comforts of assurance!"[63] Flavel, then, exhorts his reader to work hard at shoring up assurance. Notwithstanding the Spirit's role, how is this accomplished by the Christian? Why does Flavel write, "O then, give the Lord no rest, till your hearts be at rest by the assurance of his love, and the pardon of your sins"?[64] It shall be shown that Flavel maintains that several doctrinal beliefs—such as election, the covenant of grace, and union with Christ in particular—serve as the grounds for assurance while the means of grace and obedience both serve to confirm assurance. In the final analysis, all of these are meant to comfort the afflicted and console the sufferer.

Election and the Covenant of Grace as Grounds for Assurance

John Flavel understood God's sovereignty to be displayed in both eternal decree and temporal providence.[65] One aspect of this eternal decree was God's predestination of all His elect. But the way in

---

60. Flavel, *Method of Grace*, 2:126–27.
61. Flavel, *A Saint Indeed*, 5:434.
62. Flavel, *A Saint Indeed*, 5:434.
63. Flavel, *England's Duty*, 4:261. See also *Sacramental Meditations*, 6:404.
64. Flavel, *Practical Treatise of Fear*, 3:304.
65. Flavel, *Divine Conduct*, 4:426.

which God relates to His people, His elect, is by way of covenant.[66] Adam failed at the original covenant—the covenant of works—in the garden of Eden. Therefore, God initiated a covenant of grace so that His elect would be brought into a saving relationship with Him through this covenantal bond.[67] This bond had both blessings and curses based on obedience or lack thereof. However, Christ took the curses of the elect's covenant faithlessness upon Himself at the cross and remained perfectly obedient, thereby fulfilling all of the covenant obligations on behalf of the elect. The elect man or woman, then, receives this righteous position by faith alone.

Flavel taught that election is evidenced by sanctification. If an individual consistently refuses God and His call of the gospel, he or she "can by no means arrive to the evidence and assurance of…election; for your election is only secured to you by your effectual calling."[68] The only way for individuals to discern whether they are elect, and thus to attain assurance, is "by reading the work of sanctification in their own hearts."[69] According to Flavel, God's eternal election is

---

66. For an excellent study of the Puritan theology of covenant, see John von Rohr, *The Covenant of Grace in Puritan Thought* (Eugene, Ore.: Wipf & Stock, 1986). As we have seen in part in this study on Flavel and in this present section, von Rohr's analysis is certainly true of Flavel. Von Rohr writes that Puritan thought "utilized increasingly the concept of 'covenant' as a means of comprehending the human relationship with God. Although this idea, with its characteristic stress upon the bonding of parties in shared commitment, was likewise employed in some church and political circles for the structuring of social relationships, its broader usage appeared in the theological realm. God's dealing with humanity, so it was affirmed, is by way of covenant." *Covenant of Grace in Puritan Thought*, 1.

67. Flavel, *Preparation for Sufferings*, 6:80. Flavel writes extensively of various aspects related to covenant theology throughout his *Works*. In one place, for example, he writes, "In this life of dependence lies your security; and indeed this is the great difference betwixt the two *covenants*. In the first, Adam's stock was in his own hands, and so his security or misery depended upon the unconstrained choice of his own mutable and self-determining will. But now in the new covenant, all are to go to Christ, to depend upon him for supplies, and are so secured against all destructive dangers." *Preparation for Sufferings*, 6:69.

68. Flavel, *Treatise of the Soul of Man*, 3:236.

69. Flavel, *Treatise of the Soul of Man*, 3:236.

grounds for great comfort in spite of severe suffering. It serves as a ministerial doctrine to afflicted saints. "It is a matter of comfort to God's elect, amidst all dangers in the world."[70] This comfort comes, then, as the natural effect of an assurance of God's electing love. This is why Flavel can write, "If the eternal decree of God's electing love be executed, and the virtues and benefits of the death of Christ applied by the Spirit…then such a giving of the Spirit unto us must needs be a certain mark and proof of our special interest in Christ."[71]

Flavel's use of the theology of election and covenant as ministry to the suffering saint is seen clearly throughout his work *The Balm of the Covenant Applied to the Bleeding Wounds of Afflicted Saints* (c. 1687).[72] Flavel's purpose in this treatise is to comfort and minister to the sufferer by giving greater assurance in the sure and everlasting covenant of God. He explains:

> The design of the ensuing discourse, is to evince the truth of what seems a very great paradox to most men, namely, that the afflictions of the saints can do them no hurt, and that the wisdom of men and angels cannot lay one circumstance of their condition (how uneasy soever it seems to be) better, or more to their advantage than God hath laid it. I attempt not by a flourish of rhetoric to persuade you against the demonstrations you can fetch from sense and feeling to the contrary, but to overthrow the false reasonings of flesh and sense, by the allowed rules of Scripture, and sure principles of religion.[73]

Flavel is clear, moreover, that the reason sufferings can do the believer "no hurt" is because they are secured in an unbreakable bond, God's eternal covenant. This covenant gives the Christian

---

70. Flavel, *Exposition of the Assembly's Catechism*, 6:175.
71. Flavel, *Method of Grace*, 2:332. See also *England's Duty*, 4:112. Similarly, Flavel writes, "O how much is every man now concerned to have his estate and condition well cleared, and to give all diligence to make his calling and election sure!" *Touchstone of Sincerity*, 5:510.
72. The original publication date is unknown. A second edition, however, was published within Flavel's lifetime in 1688.
73. Flavel, *Balm of the Covenant*, 6:83.

great assurance of his or her salvation so that he or she might receive inner comfort amidst great suffering.

Flavel clearly attempts to minister to the suffering saint by setting forth the centrality of the covenant. For example, he writes, "Open your eyes and behold, O ye afflicted saints, all these properties of a complete relief meeting together in the covenant." He adds that the covenant "is capable of a good personal security or assurance to all God's afflicted people; for it is a *sure covenant*."[74] Flavel's desire was for his reader to find "relief and consolation…in the everlasting covenant of God."[75]

The fact that the covenant is "everlasting" means, according to Flavel, "that the benefits and mercies of the covenant are durable and endless to the peope [sic] of God."[76] Where the sufferer finds weakness, mutability, and defects within himself, he finds strength, immutability, and perfection within the covenant. This is because God's covenant is founded upon His unchangeable counsel and purpose.[77] Even still, while such a sure and everlasting covenant "secures us from the *wrath* [of God], it does not secure us from the *rod* of God."[78] In summary, Flavel writes, "The everlasting, well-ordered, and sure covenant of grace, affords everlasting, well-ordered, and sure relief to all that are within the bonds of it, how many or how great soever their personal or domestic trials and afflictions are."[79] The covenant of grace is "a complete relief and remedy to the afflicted soul" because the covenant removes and "disarms afflictions of the only stings by which they wound us," which is "the guilt of sin."[80]

We see in Flavel something of a voluntary and intentional nature of the remedy for suffering. As we have shown, Flavel understood

---

74. Flavel, *Balm of the Covenant*, 6:95–96. Elsewhere he writes, "The covenant of grace gives great security to believers." *Method of Grace*, 2:56.
75. Flavel, *Balm of the Covenant*, 6:85.
76. Flavel, *Balm of the Covenant*, 6:89. See also *Exposition of the Assembly's Catechism*, 6:176–77.
77. Flavel, *A Saint Indeed*, 5:442; *Balm of the Covenant*, 6:90.
78. Flavel, *Balm of the Covenant*, 6:91.
79. Flavel, *Balm of the Covenant*, 6:92.
80. Flavel, *Balm of the Covenant*, 6:96.

internal sufferings to be greater than external sufferings. And the internal sufferings can be relieved by being reminded and affirmed of God's secure, everlasting, and sure covenant of grace. Experiential knowledge of the covenant disarms the sting of the guilt of sin and thus brings consolation and relief to the suffering saint. The voluntary aspect is to study and apply it in all distresses. "Seeing then that the covenant of God is the great relief and support of all his afflicted people," Flavel exhorts, "Let the afflicted soul go to this blessed covenant; study and apply it in all distresses."[81] Furthermore, the covenant "alters the very nature and property of their afflictions, and turns them from a *curse* into a *blessing* to them."[82]

This last point is key to understanding Flavel's theology of suffering and his ministry to the sufferer. If he can get his reader to see that God's covenant of grace not only removes the guilt of his or her sin but turns affliction into blessing, then the natural effect is consolation, relief, and comfort. The believer, then, is to face affliction with confidence and assurance. He is to express "faith in the power, promises, and faithfulness of God, which are engaged for him in the covenant of grace, to keep him in the greatest dangers that befal him in this world."[83] Flavel's ministry to the suffering Christian finds its basis in God's covenant of grace.

Union with Christ as Ground for Assurance

The doctrine of union with Christ was vitally important in Flavel's theology.[84] By faith, Christ becomes—for the believer—his or her wisdom, righteousness, sanctification, and redemption.[85] The believer's union with Christ is intimate, permanent, and foundational to

---

81. Flavel, *Balm of the Covenant*, 6:113.
82. Flavel, *Balm of the Covenant*, 6:98.
83. Flavel, *Touchstone of Sincerity*, 5:584.
84. For an in-depth study of Flavel's doctrine of union with Christ, see Yuille, *Inner Sanctum*.
85. Cf. 1 Cor. 1:30; Flavel, *Exposition of the Assembly's Catechism*, 6:191. Yuille follows this fourfold blessing of union with Christ. See *Inner Sanctum*, 45–53.

Christian obedience and joy in God. Furthermore, Flavel explains, "It makes Christ, and all that he hath purchased, become ours."[86] Thus, we see both a positional and a relational aspect to Flavel's understanding of union with Christ. While the believer is positionally secure, he is also to grow in his relationship with Christ on the basis of that secure position. The latter is the fruit of the former.

Regarding affliction, Stephen Yuille notes, "Flavel asserts that the believer's mystical union with Christ is made evident by persevering in the midst of affliction."[87] This "persevering," Yuille contends, consists of embracing God's promises to the saints, embracing God's sovereign purposes, and embracing God's love.[88] Being united with Christ by faith provides the foundation from which the believer may grow in his or her comfort and consolation in the midst of suffering.

Union with Christ, then, naturally leads to a greater assurance of salvation. Flavel explains, "There be all the grounds and helps of assurance furnished to your hand; there is a real union betwixt Christ and your souls, which is the very ground-work of assurance."[89] Flavel calls the believer's union with Christ "the greatest and weightiest matter that can be brought to trial in this world."[90] This union, Flavel explains, is Christ's abiding with the Christian by the Spirit so that it is sincere and true, not mere "external adhesion." By "trial," Flavel refers to whether the Christian stands in Christ as a dead branch or as a living stock. In other words, the one who is united to Christ by faith will necessarily have living and active fruit from that union. When a Christian—especially a suffering Christian—sees this living and active fruit, he is to rest assured that he is indeed saved and loved by God. That he undergoes affliction, then, does not negate his union with Christ; rather, he is to grow from it and "improve" upon it by faith.

---

86. Flavel, *Exposition of the Assembly's Catechism*, 6:192.
87. Yuille, *Inner Sanctum*, 75.
88. Yuille, *Inner Sanctum*, 76–81.
89. Flavel, *Method of Grace*, 2:138.
90. Flavel, *Method of Grace*, 2:328.

According to Flavel, when a person embraces Christ by faith, he or she shall forever be with Christ. The saved soul is "Christ's habitation for ever."[91] When the elected individual receives Christ by faith, "the union is effected betwixt Christ and the soul; it is now put out of hazard."[92] Flavel writes this to minister to those who might doubt the security of salvation or who might experience various "hazards" and sufferings in life. Despite the affliction that a believer may face, "it is impossible [that] thou shouldst be lost" because of "that strict and intimate union that is betwixt Christ and thee."[93]

Flavel's desire was to encourage the suffering saint by his or her union with Christ: "Should God spare the rod of affliction, it would not be for our advantage.... All the wrath, all the curse, all the gall and wormwood was squeezed into Christ's cup, and not one drop left to imbitter ours."[94] Because the Christian is united to Christ, he is made a partaker of the benefits of union with Christ, which include great comfort, consolation, and security. Nothing in this life can take away the believer's joy in Christ. Nothing can thwart the believer's eternal salvation. Union with Christ provides the Christian, according to Flavel, a deep inner peace and joy that remain despite affliction and hardship.

The Means of Grace in Confirming Assurance

The means of God's saving grace, according to Flavel, are the ordinances of Christ, but "especially the word, sacraments, and prayer; all which are made effectual to the elect for salvation."[95] Flavel understands an ordinance to be an institution or appointment of

---

91. Flavel, *England's Duty*, 3:112.
92. Flavel, *England's Duty*, 3:113.
93. Flavel, *Preparation for Sufferings*, 6:80.
94. Flavel, *Sacramental Meditations*, 6:425.
95. Flavel, *Exposition of the Assembly's Catechism*, 6:268. This answer follows the Westminster Shorter Catechism. In several places, Flavel links these three ordinances together. See *Method of Grace*, 2:238; *England's Duty*, 4:60, 244; *Husbandry Spiritualized: The Heavenly Use of Earthly Things*, 5:38; *A Saint Indeed*, 5:508.

God. These ordinances are called "means of grace"[96] or "means of salvation" because "by them and through them the Spirit of the Lord conveys spiritual graces into men's souls."[97] Flavel calls these means the "conduits of heaven, from whence grace is watered and made fruitful."[98] While God can certainly convert men and women without these means, "they are the ordinary standing means." They, of course, are made effectual only for the elect, and none other.[99] That these means of grace strengthen assurance in the sufferer is part and parcel of Flavel's ministry to those suffering.

Assurance and Comfort from the Bible

The Bible figures prominently in Flavel's thought concerning both the salvation and sanctification of God's elect. In the face of affliction and hardship, the believer can have confidence upon God's promises as revealed in the Bible: "He builds this confidence…upon the promises of God, which are his security in future dangers."[100] He writes elsewhere of how the Scriptures attest to one's salvation by revealing the proper "signs of faith," thereby bringing greater assurance of one's salvation. He explains, "You have the scriptures before you which contain the signs of faith, and the very things within you that answer those signs in the word."[101] The Bible, according to Flavel, "must be applied for our comfort in all inward and outward troubles."[102]

---

96. While in his *Exposition of the Assembly's Catechism* Flavel uses the phrase "means of salvation," he frequently uses the phrase "means of grace" throughout his *Works*. See *Fountain of Life*, 1:27, 290, 403; *Method of Grace*, 2:43, 129, 140, 259, 439, 443, 445; *Treatise of the Soul of Man*, 2:587; *England's Duty*, 4:48, 109, 137; *Husbandry Spiritualized*, 5:64; *Preparation for Sufferings*, 6:40. Moreover, he often differentiates these as "external means" as distinguished from the work of the Holy Spirit, applying the spiritual benefits of these external means.
97. Flavel, *Exposition of the Assembly's Catechism*, 6:268.
98. Flavel, *A Saint Indeed*, 5:436.
99. Flavel, *Exposition of the Assembly's Catechism*, 6:269.
100. Flavel, *Touchstone of Sincerity*, 5:584.
101. Flavel, *Method of Grace*, 2:138.
102. Flavel, *Exposition of the Assembly's Catechism*, 6:274.

It should also be noted that Flavel inserts Scripture on just about every page throughout his *Works*. Not only does he desire to ground his doctrine in the Bible, but he also uses it as a way to confirm what he believes about Scripture—that it is a means by which God increases the believer's faith and comforts the suffering saint. For example, in his *Exposition of the Assembly's Catechism*, he goes through each question of the Westminster Shorter Catechism and then adds a series of questions of his own, each answer containing biblical references. Why? Because Flavel affirmed that Scripture must be applied to believers, and to suffering believers, that they might find comfort amidst affliction.[103]

Assurance and Comfort from Prayer

In accord with Scripture, Flavel taught that prayer is a means by which God comforts the afflicted. Flavel understood prayer to be the "best way" for the Christian "to ease his heart when surcharged with sorrow."[104] He exhorts his reader to "follow every affliction with prayer, that God would follow it with his blessing."[105] Elsewhere, he writes, "Blessed be God for the ordinance of prayer; how much are all the saints beholden to it, at all times, but especially in heart-sinking and distressful times?"[106] Prayer is not only a right response to suffering but also a means by which the sufferer may find comfort and blessing in God's grace. For Flavel, "The door of grace is opened by the key of prayer."[107]

Because of the believer's union with Christ and the security found in the covenant of grace, the believer is to seek grace to come to God in prayer with full assurance of faith. Prayer, in turn, increases the assurance and faith of the believer.[108] Flavel wants his reader to find comfort in prayer in the midst of affliction:

---

103. Flavel, *Exposition of the Assembly's Catechism*, 6:274.
104. Flavel, *Preparation for Sufferings*, 6:64.
105. Flavel, *Method of Grace*, 2:390.
106. Flavel, *Token for Mourners*, 5:664.
107. Flavel, *Method of Grace*, 2:263.
108. Flavel, *Exposition of the Assembly's Catechism*, 6:294–95, 315.

> Consider how all the troubles in this world would be sweetened, and all your burdens lightened, if once your souls were in Christ, and in covenant with God. O what heart's ease would faith give you! What sweet relief would you find in prayer! These things…would suddenly cool, relieve, and ease your spirits; could you but go to God as a Father, and pour out your hearts before him, and cast all your cares and burdens, wants and sorrows upon him; you would find a speedy out-let to your troubles, and an inlet to all peace, all comforts, and all refreshments.[109]

From this, we can see how prayer naturally leads to greater comfort and peace even in the midst of troubles and affliction. Flavel further guides his reader in this ordinance of prayer by urging, "Be much with God in secret, open your hearts to him, and pour out your complaints into his bosom…. Plead hard with God in prayer for help and healing."[110]

Prayer strengthens confidence and faith, which in turn builds up assurance and joy in salvation.[111] This, then, brings about comfort and consolation in suffering. "Pray earnestly for the sanctification of all your troubles to your eternal good…be more earnest with God, rather to have your troubles sanctified than prevented."[112] Prayer is a way, Flavel teaches, for the believer to resign himself into the greater wisdom and sovereignty of God. Thus "suffering times are resigning times."[113] God's sovereignty should encourage the Christian to commit him or herself into His hands, and trust Him over all.[114] Flavel understood prayer to be the means by which the believer could gain greater faith and assurance in his or her salvation. As Flavel reiterates, this brings support and comfort in time

---

109. Flavel, *Treatise of the Soul of Man*, 3:199–200. See also *Practical Treatise on Fear*, 3:298; *Divine Conduct*, 4:433.
110. Flavel, *Method of Grace*, 2:200.
111. Flavel, *Vindiciarum Vindex*, 3:541. See also *England's Duty*, 4:300.
112. Flavel, *Righteous Man's Refuge*, 3:408.
113. Flavel, *Righteous Man's Refuge*, 3:408.
114. Flavel, *Righteous Man's Refuge*, 3:409.

of need: "Prayer is the out-let of the saints sorrows, and the in-let of their supports and comforts."[115]

Assurance and Comfort from the Sacraments

In addition to the Bible and prayer, Flavel maintains that the sacraments—especially the sacrament of the Lord's Supper—strengthen the faith and assurance of the believer. This is particularly true for the suffering believer. He writes, "Improve well your sacrament seasons, those harvest days of faith: This ordinance hath a direct and peculiar tendency to the improvement and strengthening of faith.... By this seal also the promise comes to be more ratified to us; and the firmer the promise appears to the soul, the more bold and adventurous faith is in casting itself upon it; Oh! how many poor, doubting, trembling souls have, in such a season, gathered the full ripe fruits of assurance from the top-boughs of that ordinance!"[116] This passage makes it clear that Flavel understood the sacraments to be direct means by which God strengthens faith and thus strengthens assurance as well.

In his treatise on the Lord's Supper, *Sacramental Meditations*, Flavel exhorts his reader to prepare for this sacrament by meditating upon the sufferings of Christ, so as to bring about greater assurance of one's salvation: "Infer from the sufferings of Christ, those conclusions of faith that tend to assurance."[117] It is the believer's duty to "improve all ordinances, especially this great sealing ordinance [the Lord's Supper], for your farther confirmation and establishment."[118] By both preparing and taking the Lord's Supper, the Christian is to grow in assurance of his or her salvation. This assurance, then, is to lead to greater comfort for the sufferer. The Lord's Supper brings

---

115. Flavel, *England's Duty*, 4:249. Similarly, he writes, "Do not neglect prayer when straits befal you. You see it is Providence dispenses all, you live upon it; therefore apply yourselves to God in the times of need." *Divine Conduct*, 4:398.
116. Flavel, *Preparation for Sufferings*, 6:45.
117. Flavel, *Sacramental Meditations*, 6:455.
118. Flavel, *Sacramental Meditations*, 6:410.

Christ to the believer and he or she is to learn from Christ in His sufferings. The result? "O that you would learn to be more Christ-like in all your trials and afflictions!... O that such would *behold the Lamb of God*, as represented in this ordinance!"[119]

As "means of salvation," Flavel intends "our complete and final deliverance from sin and misery, both temporal and eternal."[120] This does not mean, to be sure, that the sacraments in themselves save, but rather that God ordinarily works in and through them—along with the preaching of the Word and prayer—to bring about saving grace. While the Word, in particular, is God's means to "beget faith," the sacraments are "to seal and confirm it."[121] Thus we see that Flavel understands the sacraments to be a means by which God strengthens faith and confirms His promises to the believer.

Christian Obedience in Confirming Assurance

Flavel held that the believer could experience greater assurance of his or her salvation by sheer obedience to God. In fact, obedience is necessary for Christian assurance. He writes, "Assurance is unattainable without obedience; we can never be comfortable Christians except we be strict and regular Christians."[122] How can this be? Flavel explains that faith increases through acts of obedience; it leads to an improvement of the grace applied by the Holy Spirit. In other words, "faith improves by obedience." As "diligence in the work of God is the direct way to the assurance of the love of God," so also it is a path that "leads you into a heaven upon earth."[123] Even when—or especially when—the believer is doubtful of God's love in times of trials and suffering, he or she should be all the more diligent to pursue obedience to God. This confirms his or her assurance of salvation.

According to Flavel, the effects of obedience leading to assurance are peace and relief in times of trouble. The Christian's internal

---

119. Flavel, *Sacramental Meditations*, 6:416–17.
120. Flavel, *Exposition of the Assembly's Catechism*, 6:276.
121. Flavel, *Exposition of the Assembly's Catechism*, 6:276, 279, 286.
122. Flavel, *Method of Grace*, 2:401.
123. Flavel, *Method of Grace*, 2:408.

convictions over doing what is right, and then followed and obeyed, "are the inlets to Christ, and eternal salvation by him." Flavel adds, "Till you obey and yield up yourselves to them, Christ is shut out of your souls; he knocks, but finds no entrance."[124] By this, Flavel is not reverting to salvation by works; rather, he is conveying the idea that the believer will have greater communion with Christ through obedience. This obedience, in turn, confirms assurance, which leads to peace and relief.

It should be pointed out that Flavel emphasized obedience with the promised comforts of assurance. While obeying God's commands is certainly a key theme in Flavel's writings, he often dovetails obedience and the benefits that spring from it. One of the greatest duties of a Christian that leads to assurance is attending to the heart, or, as Flavel puts it, "keeping the heart." He warns against neglecting the sin-filled heart and that such neglect leads to greater expressions of outward sin. "He that is negligent in attending his own heart, is (ordinarily) a great stranger to assurance, and the sweet comforts flowing from it."[125] Or, put another way, "God doth not usually indulge lazy and negligent souls with the comforts of assurance."[126]

The assurance that grows out of Christian obedience provides a right understanding for affliction when it arises. Confirmed by obedience, assurance changes the perspective of affliction as evil to affliction as blessing. Flavel writes, "O how many have been coached to hell in the chariots of earthly pleasures, while others have been whipped to heaven by the rod of affliction!"[127] Indeed, "they are mistaken that think the beautiful child of assurance may be born without pangs."[128] It is clear that Flavel believed that obedience leads the believer into greater faith, which leads to greater assurance of his or her salvation. In this way, obedience confirms and establishes assurance for the Christian, especially the suffering Christian.

---

124. Flavel, *England's Duty*, 4:297.
125. Flavel, *A Saint Indeed*, 5:433.
126. Flavel, *A Saint Indeed*, 5:435.
127. Flavel, *A Saint Indeed*, 5:438.
128. Flavel, *A Saint Indeed*, 5:435.

Conclusion and Analysis

For Flavel, "Trials are the high way to assurance."[129] By helping his suffering reader to see personal suffering from this different perspective, he hoped to provide some relief and comfort as a minister. Not only did Flavel desire the suffering Christian to pursue assurance as a duty, but also he sought to minister to his reader's pain by pointing to the comforts and joys that flow out of assurance.

To return to Beeke's analysis and codification of Westminster's teaching on the doctrine of assurance, Flavel certainly agrees with the theology as articulated in the Westminster Confession of Faith. In particular, we have seen that Flavel understood the work of assurance to be placed primarily in the work of the Holy Spirit. Second, Flavel understood the doctrine of decretal election and the covenant of grace to be sources of and grounds for great assurance for the suffering Christian. Third, Flavel believed that the doctrine of union with Christ—and the outworking of communion with Him—to be grounds for Christian assurance. Fourth, Flavel taught that the means of grace—the Word, prayer, and sacraments in particular—as well as obedience to God's commands are necessary ways in which the believer may confirm his or her assurance of salvation. Flavel's goal in writing on these topics to the Christian sufferer, then, was to bring relief and consolation to his or her pain. In this way, affliction could be turned into "a high way to assurance."

---

129. Flavel, *Touchstone of Sincerity*, 5:581.

CHAPTER SEVEN

The Cessation of Suffering in Flavel's Ministry to Sufferers

That the afflictions in this world will soon pass, according to Flavel, offers great comfort, consolation, and hope to the suffering Christian. Flavel sought to minister to the suffering believer by teaching the importance of seeing this present life—with all of its trials and pains—as a temporary existence that foreshadowed an eternal existence in heaven. In other words, the affliction experienced in this life is but momentary and by God's eternal design. Flavel wanted his suffering reader to know that "the time of your relief and full deliverance from all your troubles is at hand."[1] By being "at hand," Flavel desired his reader to continually look ahead with positive hope for the end of suffering and the sinless joys of heaven.[2]

This Momentary Affliction

As seen in the previous chapters, Flavel believed that the existence of suffering is ordained by God and used in His infinite wisdom for His glory. But God also ordains the limits of that suffering as well. Flavel writes, "In all the evils of trouble and afflictions that befal you, eye Jesus Christ.... He elects the instrument of your trouble; he makes the rod as afflictive as he pleaseth; he orders the continuance and end of your troubles; and they will not cease to be afflictive to

---

1. Flavel, *Method of Grace*, 2:413.
2. "At hand" did not necessarily mean that Christ's return was actually very soon. Rather, while it *could* be soon, Flavel saw himself and his contemporaries living in an age—since the first century—that understood itself to be watching and waiting for the second advent of Christ.

you, till Christ say, Leave off, it is enough."³ As God is sovereign over the duration and extent of the believer's suffering, He is also sovereign over the end or cessation of that suffering.

It is clear that the purpose of Flavel's writing on the cessation of suffering was to minister to the suffering believer. He explains, "All your calamities will have an end shortly.... Let that support your hearts under all your sufferings."⁴ It brings great consolation to the suffering believer to know that suffering is limited. In writing of God's sovereignty over the boundaries of our suffering, Flavel exclaims, "O my soul! What marrow and fatness, comfort and consolation mayest thou suck from the breast of this truth in the darkest day of trouble?"⁵ As if to make it all the more memorable, Flavel puts this desire in a poem:

> This world's a forest, where, from day to day,
> Bears, wolves, and lions, range and seek their prey;
> Amidst them all poor harmless lambs are fed,
> And by their very dens in safety led.
> They roar upon us, but are held in chains;
> Our shepherd is their keeper, he maintains
> Our lot. Why then should we so trembling stand?
> We meet them, true, but in their keeper's hand.
> He that to raging seas such bounds hath put,
> The mouths of rav'nous beasts can also shut.
> Sleep in the woods, poor lambs, yourselves repose
> Upon his care, whose eyes do never close.⁶

Healing comes to the Christian sufferer from the knowledge that affliction ultimately will cease, and this is a central theme in Flavel's pastoral writings. He puts forth two ways in which this suffering will end: in duration and in operation. He explains suffering's duration and operation when he writes, "Look forward, to the end of your troubles; yea, look to a double end of them, the end of their *duration*,

---

3. Flavel, *Fountain of Life*, 1:221–22.
4. Flavel, *Divine Conduct*, 4:488.
5. Flavel, *Navigation Spiritualized*, 5:255.
6. Flavel, *Navigation Spiritualized*, 5:255.

and the end of their *operation*."[7] By duration, Flavel seeks to prove his point that suffering is not everlasting for the Christian. To support this, he quotes from 2 Corinthians 4:17, "For our light affliction, which is but for a moment, worketh for us a far more exceeding and eternal weight of glory."[8] Affliction, as a spoonful of water, will surely come to an end in the sea of eternity: "These afflictions are but *temporal*...but Christ and his benefits are *eternal*."[9] Such a perspective, according to Flavel, makes the sufferings experienced in this life relatively small compared to the "exceeding weight of glory," which will be experienced in the world to come.[10] This comparison is an important element in Flavel's ministry to sufferers. He rhetorically asks his reader, "Is not eternal life worth the suffering of a moment's pain?"[11] Helping his reader to see the comparatively small suffering in this life to the eternal glory and blessedness of the life to come is one specific way in which Flavel seeks to minister to the suffering believer.

But suffering is also temporary in its operation. By this, Flavel means the effects of suffering. The effects, for the believer, actually turn to blessing and are therefore of a temporary nature. In this way, "Christ cures outward *troubles* by inward *consolations*, which are made to rise in the inner man as high as the waters of affliction do upon the outward man."[12] By affliction, Flavel argues, Christians are made partakers of Christ's holiness; sin is removed, and happiness is perfected.[13]

---

7. Flavel, *Fountain of Life*, 1:367.
8. Flavel, *Fountain of Life*, 1:367.
9. Flavel, *Method of Grace*, 2:73. See also *A Saint Indeed*, 5:449.
10. Flavel, *Fountain of Life*, 1:368. Similarly, he writes, "You shall enjoy the pure, divine, suitable and everlasting pleasures of holiness. Consider now, and accordingly make your choice, whether you will take the pleasures of sin, which are but for a season, in exchange for the everlasting joys which are at God's right hand for ever." *England's Duty*, 4:135.
11. Flavel, *A Saint Indeed*, 5:488. Similarly, he writes, "Take notice of the approaches of *eternity*: remember you are almost at the end of time: and when you come to launch out in that endless ocean, how will these things look then?" *Preparation for Sufferings*, 5:55.
12. Flavel, *Method of Grace*, 2:195.
13. Flavel, *Fountain of Life*, 1:368.

In both its duration and operation, suffering will come to an end. The knowledge of and faith in this fact, according to Flavel, provide the suffering Christian with great comfort and relief in his affliction. If the Christian knows and believes that this present world with all its troubles is but momentary, he or she can have greater perseverance, joy, and hope in the midst of any affliction.

The Last Resurrection and the Hope of Heaven

Flavel also seeks to minister to the suffering believer by pointing out two great truths: (1) the believer's final bodily resurrection, and (2) the hope of heaven. When Flavel discusses the inherently temporary nature of the Christian's suffering, these two positive elements are the other side of the coin. In fact, they add to and strengthen Flavel's argument that the afflicted Christian can find great comfort in the midst of outward trials.

The Last Resurrection

Flavel taught from Scripture that when Christ returns, the bodies of believers will be raised and reunited to their souls.[14] At death, the souls of Christians immediately go to be with Jesus in heaven. But at Christ's second advent, their bodies and souls will be reunited. Thus death—while it ushers the believer into the bliss of a sinless life with Christ—is incomplete. Iain Murray, in *The Puritan Hope*, writes of the Puritan conception of this in-between state: "Death is gain and paradise for the individual believer, yet the bliss is incomplete. As long as the soul is separated from the body the believer is only in an intermediate state; he must await resurrection, glorification and full redemption."[15] Flavel uses this belief to minister to the suffering saint: "The hope of the resurrection should powerfully restrain all excesses of sorrow in those that do profess it." Why? Because "death is but a longer sleep, out of which [Christians] shall as surely

---

14. Flavel, *Fountain of Life*, 1:529.
15. Iain Murray, *The Puritan Hope: Revival and the Interpretation of Prophecy* (Edinburgh: Banner of Truth, 1971), 215.

awake."[16] Flavel points to the consolation of this doctrine as "the comfortable, and heart-supporting doctrine of the resurrection."[17]

The resurrection of the body at Christ's second coming, according to Flavel, should delight the suffering saint. In writing of a mother whose son had died, Flavel ministers with these words: "The resurrection of her son from the dead, is the ground upon which Christ builds her consolation, and relief; well might he say, *Weep not*, when he intended quickly to remove the cause of her tears, by restoring him again to life."[18] Or, to put it another way, Flavel writes, "It remains, then, that the ground of all solid comfort and relief... lies in the general and last resurrection."[19] How is the Christian's resurrection a "ground" of comfort and relief? According to Flavel, it is directly tied to the resurrection of Jesus.

The basis of the believer's resurrection, and thus his or her comfort, rests in the fact that Christ Himself was raised to life. Flavel explains, "As sure as Christ arose the third day, notwithstanding the seal and watch that were upon him; so sure the church shall arise out of all her troubles."[20] The last resurrection points back to the resurrection of Christ and also to the believer's union with Christ. If Christ was raised to life, then the believer also will be raised to life. Though troubles in this world threaten to kill and destroy, they cannot do so permanently. The resurrection of the body shall overcome even death itself.

The Hope of Heaven

On the heels of the resurrection is the full and complete joy of heaven. By pointing his reader to the celestial city, Flavel sought to bring hope and comfort to the suffering believer. In his chapter "The Puritan Death-bed," Ralph Houlbrooke writes that the Puritan understanding of life was a preparation for heaven. He

---

16. Flavel, *Token for Mourners*, 5:638.
17. Flavel, *Token for Mourners*, 5:639.
18. Flavel, *Token for Mourners*, 5:610.
19. Flavel, *Token for Mourners*, 5:612.
20. Flavel, *A Saint Indeed*, 5:449.

explains, "Earthly life was a long process of dying. Its most important aim should be to prepare oneself for the far more important life hereafter."[21] Similarly, Iain Murray writes of the Puritan understanding of the transitory nature of this earthly life, "This world will never be the Church's rest."[22] In other words, death was an entry point to heaven, which is the true home of the believer.

Even at the point of the greatest suffering or death of a Christian, Flavel taught that a believer should perceive such affliction very differently from the way a nonbeliever would. He urges his readers to consider the immediate bliss of heaven at death: "Farewell vain world, with all the mixed and imperfect comforts of it, and welcome the more sweet, suitable, and satisfying company of Father, Son, and Spirit, holy angels, and perfected saints."[23] While this world offers "imperfect comforts," heaven will bring an all-satisfying and eternal comfort. It is heaven, Flavel argues, that suffering believers should desire, and on eternity that they ought to fix their gaze. Flavel goes so far as to encourage his Christian reader to keep an eye toward heaven throughout the whole course of life, not only in times of suffering. By doing this, Flavel contends, affection for things in this world will fade and so too will affliction. In writing of the love for this world, he admonishes, "It is a strong affection that makes strong affliction."[24]

This sentiment is similar to what Iain Murray sees as a division between how the Puritan was to view the world to come while still living in the "trials" of the world now. In capturing the Puritan understanding of living with a view of the afterlife, he writes, "The wonders of the world to come are not revealed to us in order that we may live our present lives in sadness, asking how much longer this must last."[25] In other words, the Puritan attitude was not to be one of gloom and despair, but quite the contrary. The hope of heaven

---

21. Houlbrooke, "Puritan Death-bed," 129.
22. Murray, *Puritan Hope*, 218.
23. Flavel, *Treatise of the Soul of Man*, 2:586–87.
24. Flavel, *Divine Conduct*, 4:430.
25. Murray, *Puritan Hope*, 218.

was to draw the Puritan into a greater ability to endure suffering in this life with patience, joy, and hope.

According to Flavel, the affection of Christians should be drawn to heaven, especially in times of affliction. On the other hand, unbelievers have only "eternal damnation" ahead because they stand as condemned persons with "no promise to entitle…any mercy."[26] Flavel wants his reader to see the stark difference between the hope of heaven for the believer and the judgment of hell for the unbeliever. While the unbeliever stands eternally condemned, the Christian has enough mercy in salvation alone "to sweeten all your troubles in this world."[27]

Flavel maintains that the suffering believer should see his or her suffering in comparison to the joy and hope of heaven. He explains, "But O what a transcendent joy, yea, ravishing, will over-run the hearts of saints, when, after so many conflicts, temptations, and afflictions, they arrive in glory, and are harboured in heaven, where they shall rest for ever!… Many a hard storm they ride out, and many straits and troubles they here encounter with, but at last they arrive at their desired and long-expected haven, and then heaven rings and resounds with their joyful acclamations."[28] The afflictions of this life, according to Flavel, should be seen in light of the eternal rest and joy of heaven. In this way, Flavel offers comfort and hope to the suffering Christian.

Conclusion and Analysis

One way in which Flavel seeks to minister to the suffering believer is to explain that the affliction experienced in this life is not only momentary but also will fade before the eternal hope and joy of heaven. The consolation of viewing suffering as merely momentary and as "insignificant" compared to the eternal weight of glory in

---

26. Flavel, *Divine Conduct*, 4:431.
27. Flavel, *Divine Conduct*, 4:432.
28. Flavel, *Navigation Spiritualized*, 5:290. See also *A Saint Indeed*, 5:461 and *Preparation for Sufferings*, 6:55.

heaven are but two sides of the same coin. Not only will suffering come to an end, Flavel argues, but it will also be translated into eternal bliss and full satisfaction. However, that does not mean that his suffering reader should simply venture through life with sadness and gloom over earthly troubles. Rather, Flavel maintains that the hope of heaven should lift his soul to endure afflictions in the world with greater patience and joy.

Flavel is careful to point his Christian readers to their resurrection as a confirmation of their union with Christ and, thus, of their communion with Him for eternity. The intended effect of Flavel's words of consolation is to bring the afflicted believer a heavenly vision and strength to endure the sufferings of this present world. No matter how dark and heavy earthly anxieties may seem, they are light compared to the weight of glory and joy in the world to come.

Bibliography

Affleck, Bert. "The Theology of Richard Sibbes, 1577–1635." PhD diss., Drew University, 1968.

Alexander, James W. *The Life of Archibald Alexander, D.D.* Harrisonburg, Va.: Sprinkle Publications, 1991.

Allestree, Richard. *The Art of Patience under All Afflictions: An Appendix to* The Art of Contentment. *By the Author of* The Whole Duty of Man. London: Printed for W. Cademan in the Lower-Walk of the New Exchange, in the Strands, 1684.

Banvard, Joseph. *Golden Gems for the Christian, Selected from the Writings of Rev. John Flavel; With a Memoir of the Author.* Boston: Gould and Lincoln, 1848.

Battles, Ford Lewis. *Interpreting John Calvin.* Edited by Robert Benedetto. Grand Rapids: Baker, 1996.

Beeke, Joel R. *The Quest for Full Assurance: The Legacy of Calvin and His Successors.* Edinburgh: Banner of Truth, 1999.

———. *A Reader's Guide to Reformed Literature: An Annotated Bibliography of Reformed Theology.* Grand Rapids: Reformation Heritage Books, 1999.

———, and Randall J. Pederson. *Meet the Puritans.* Grand Rapids: Reformation Heritage Books, 2006.

Bennett, James, and David Bogue. *History of Dissenters, from the Revolution in 1688, to the Year 1808.* London: Williams and Smith, 1809.

Bogue, David, and James Bennett. *History of Dissenters, from the Revolution to the Year 1838.* London: Tentmaker Publications, 2000.

Boland, Michael. Publisher's introduction to *The Mystery of Providence,* by John Flavel. Edinburgh: Banner of Truth, 1963.

Bonar, Andrew A. *Diary and Letters*. London: Hodder and Stoughton, 1884.

Boone, Clifford B. "Puritan Evangelism: Preaching for Conversion in Late Seventeenth-Century English Puritanism as Seen in the Works of John Flavel." PhD diss., University of Wales, Lampeter, 2009.

Boston, Thomas. *The Crook in the Lot; Or, the Sovereignty and Wisdom of God in the Afflictions of Men*. Glasgow, 1752.

Bray, Gerald, ed. *Documents of the English Reformation*. Cambridge: James Clarke & Co., 1994.

Bremer, Francis J. *Puritanism: A Very Short Introduction*. Oxford: Oxford University Press, 2009.

———, and Tom Webster, eds. *Puritans and Puritanism in Europe and America: A Comprehensive Encyclopedia*. Santa Barbara, Calif.: ABC-CLIO, 2006.

Bridge, William. *A Lifting Up for the Downcast*. London: Printed by Peter Cole, at the Sign of the Printing-Press in Cornhil, by the Exchange, 1649.

Brook, Benjamin. *The Lives of the Puritans, Containing a Biographical Account of Those Divines Who Distinguished Themselves in the Cause of Religious Liberty*. 3 vols. London, 1813.

Bunyan, John. *The Miscellaneous Works of John Bunyan*. Edited by Roger Sharrock and Owen C. Watkins. 12 vols. Oxford: Oxford University Press, 1988.

———. *The Works of John Bunyan*. Edited by George Offor. 3 vols. Glasgow: W. G. Blackie and Son, 1854. Reprint, Edinburgh: Banner of Truth, 1991.

Burroughs, Jeremiah. *The Rare Jewel of Christian Contentment Wherein Is Shewed, I. What Contentment Is, II. The Holy Art or Mystery of It, III. Several Lessons That Christ Teacheth, to Work the Heart to Contentment, IV. The Excellencies of It, V. The Evils of Murmuring, VII. The Aggravations of the Sin of Murmuring. By Jeremiah Burroughs*. London: Printed for Peter Cole at the Printing-Press in Cornhil, near the Royall Exchange, 1649.

Calamy, Edmund. *The Nonconformist's Memorial: Being an Account of the Ministers, Who Were Ejected or Silenced after the Restoration, Particularly by the Act of Uniformity, Which Took Place

Bibliography

on *Bartholomew-Day, August 24, 1662*. London: Printed for W. Harris, 1775.

Calhoun, David B. *The Life, Books and Influence of John Bunyan*. Ross-Shire, Scotland: CFP Mentor, 2005.

Calvin, John. *The Institutes of the Christian Religion*. Edited by John T. McNeill. Translated by Ford Lewis Battles. Philadelphia: Westminster John Knox, 1960.

Chang, Kwai Sing. "John Flavel of Dartmouth, 1630–1691." PhD diss., University of Edinburgh, 1952.

Charnock, Stephen. *A Discourse of Divine Providence*. Ames, Iowa: International Outreach, 2005.

Coffey, John. *Persecution and Toleration in Protestant England, 1558–1689*. Studies in Modern History. Harlow, U.K.: Longman Publishing Group, 2000.

———, and Paul C. H. Lim, eds. *The Cambridge Companion to Puritanism*. Cambridge: Cambridge University Press, 2008.

Cole, Benjamin. *Authentic Extracts from the Lives of John Flavel and Rev. William Tennent*. Vermont, 1807.

Collinson, Patrick. *English Puritanism*. London: The Historical Association, 1983.

———. *From Cramner to Sancroft*. London: Hambledon Continuum, 2006.

Cook, Paul E. G. Review of *The Works of John Flavel*. *The Evangelical Quarterly* 41, no. 3 (July–September 1969): 178–80.

Cosby, Brian. "The Christology of John Flavel." *Puritan Reformed Journal* 4, no. 1 (January 2012): 116–34.

———. "John Flavel: The Lost Puritan." *Puritan Reformed Journal* 3, no. 1 (January 2011): 113–32.

———. "Toward a Definition of 'Puritan' and 'Puritanism': A Study in Puritan Historiography." *Churchman* 122, no. 4 (Winter 2008): 297–314.

Cragg, Gerald R. *Puritanism in the Period of the Great Persecution, 1660–1688*. Cambridge: Cambridge University Press, 1957.

Dallimore, Arnold A. *George Whitefield: The Life and Times of the Great Evangelist of the Eighteenth-Century Revival*. Edinburgh: Banner of Truth, 1980.

Davies, Michael. *Graceful Readings: Theology and Narrative in the Works of John Bunyan*. Oxford: Oxford University Press, 2002.

Deckard, Mark. *Helpful Truth in Past Places: The Puritan Practice of Biblical Counseling*. Ross-Shire, Scotland: Christian Focus Publications, 2009.

Dever, Mark E. "Richard Sibbes and the 'Truly Evangelicall Church of England': A Study in Reformed Divinity and Early Stuart Conformity." PhD diss., University of Cambridge, 1992.

"Devonshire and the Indulgence of 1672." London: The Congregational Historical Society, 1901.

Dickens, A. G. *The English Reformation*. 2nd ed. University Park, Pa.: Pennsylvania State University Press, 1989.

Dunan-Page, Ann. *Grace Overwhelming: John Bunyan, The Pilgrim's Progress and the Extremes of the Baptist Mind*. Frankfurt: Peter Lang, 2006.

Duncan, Ligon, ed. *The Westminster Confession into the Twenty-First Century*. Ross-Shire, Scotland: Christian Focus Publications, 2003.

Durston, Christopher, and Jacqueline Eales. *The Culture of English Puritanism*. New York: Palgrave Macmillan, 1996.

Edwards, Jonathan. *On Religious Affections*. Vol. 1 of *The Works of Jonathan Edwards*. Edinburgh: Banner of Truth, 1974.

Embry, Adam Burgess. "John Flavel's Theology of the Holy Spirit." *The Southern Baptist Journal of Theology* 14, no. 4 (Winter 2010): 84–99.

———. "Keeper of the Great Seal of Heaven: Sealing of the Spirit in the Thought of John Flavel." ThM thesis, The Southern Baptist Theological Seminary, 2008.

———. *Keeper of the Great Seal of Heaven: Sealing of the Spirit in the Thought of John Flavel*. Grand Rapids: Reformation Heritage Books, 2011.

Everson, Don Marvin. "The Puritan Theology of John Owen." ThD diss., The Southern Baptist Theological Seminary, 1959.

Farrell, Earl T. "The Doctrine of Man and Grace as Held by the Reverend John Flavel." BD thesis, Duke University, 1949.

Ferguson, Sinclair. "The Doctrine of the Christian Life in the Teaching of Dr John Owen." PhD diss., University of Aberdeen, 1979.

Ferrell, Frank E. "Richard Sibbes: A Study in Early Seventeenth Century English Puritanism." PhD diss., University of Edinburgh, 1955.

Fiering, Norman S. *Moral Philosophy at Seventeenth-Century Harvard: A Discipline in Transition*. Chapel Hill: University of North Carolina Press, 1981.

Flavel, John. *The Balm of the Covenant Applied to the Bleeding Wounds of Afflicted Saints, First Composed for the Relief of a Pious and Worthy Family, Mourning over the Deaths of Their Hopeful Children; And Now Made Publick for the Support of All Christians, Sorrowing on the Same or Any Other Account. To Which Is Added, A Sermon Preached for the Funeral of That Excellent and Religious Gentleman John Upton of Lupton, esq.* 2nd ed. London: Printed for J. Harris, at the Harrow against the Church in the Poultrey, 1688.

———. *Divine Conduct; Or, The Mysterie of Providence. Wherein the Being and Efficacy of Providence is Asserted and Vindicated; The Methods of Providence As It Passes through the Several Stages of Our Lives Opened; And the Proper Course of Improving All Providences Directed, in a Treatise upon Psalm 57. Ver. 2.* London: Printed by R. W. for Francis Tyton at the Three Daggers in Fleetstreet, 1678.

———. *The Fountain of Life Opened Up; Or, A Display of Christ in His Essential and Mediatorial Glory*. London: Printed by Rob. White, for Francis Tyton, at the Three Daggers in Fleetstreet, 1673.

———. *Husbandry Spiritualized, Or, The Heavenly Use of Earthly Things, Consisting of Many Pleasant Observations, Pertinent Applications and Serious Reflections, and Each Chapter Concluded with a Divine and Suitable Poem Directing Husband-men to the Most Excellent Improvements of Their Common Imployments: Whereunto Are Added, by Way of Appendix, Several Choice Occasional Meditations, upon Birds, Beasts, Trees, Flowers, Rivers, and Several Other Objects Fitted for the Help of Such As Desire to Walk with God in All Their Solitudes and Recesses from the World*. London: Printed and Are to Be Sold by Robert Boulter, 1669.

———. *The Method of Grace, in Bringing Home the Eternal Redemption Contrived by the Father, and Accomplished by the Son through* the *Effectual Application of the Spirit unto God's Elect, Being the Second Part of Gospel Redemption: Wherein the Great Mysterie of Our Union and Communion with Christ Is Opened and Applied, Unbelievers Invited, False Pretenders Convicted, Every Man's Claim to Christ Examined, and the Misery of Christless Persons Discovered and Bewailed.* London: Printed by M. White, for Francis Tyton at Three Daggers in Fleetstreet near the Inner-Temple-Gate, 1681.

———. *A New Compass for Seamen Consisting of XXXII Points of Pleasant Observations, Profitable Applications, and Serious Reflections, All Concluded with So Many Spiritual Poems, Directing Them to Stear Their True Course to Heaven, and to Avoid the Dangerous Rocks on Either Side: Containing Many Things of Singular Use for All Christians, Especially for Such As Go Down into the Sea, and Do Business in the Great Waters.* London: Printed for the Author, sold by Rich. Tomlins, 1664.

———. *Preparation for Sufferings; Or, The Best Work in the Worst Times Wherein the Necessity, Excellency, and Means of Our Readiness for Sufferings Are Evinced and Prescribed; Our Call to Suffering Cleared, and the Great Unreadiness of Many Professours Bewailed.* London: Printed for Robert Boulter at the Turks-head in Cornhil, 1681.

———. *A Token for Mourners: Or, The Advice of Christ to a Distressed Mother, Bewailing the Death of Her Dear and Only Son. Wherein, The Boundaries of Sorrow Are Duly Fixed, Excesses Restrained, the Common Pleas Answered, and Divers Rules for the Support of Gods Afflicted Ones Prescribed.* Turks-head in Cornhill, over against the Royal Exchange, 1674.

———. *The Whole Works of the Reverend Mr. John Flavel, Late Minister at Dartmouth in Devon, in Two Volumes.* London: Parkhurst, Newman, Bell and Cockerill, 1701.

———. *The Works of John Flavel.* London: W. Baynes and Son, 1820. Reprint, London: Banner of Truth, 1968.

———, and Isaac Watts. *The Sinner Directed to the Saviour.* London: Printed by Augustus Applegath and Edward Cowper for the Religious Tract Society; Sold by F. Collins and J. Nisbet, 1820.

Flavel[l], Phinehas. *The Grand Evil Discovered, or, The Deceitfull Heart Tryed and Cast; Being the Substance of Some Sermons Preached from Jerem. XVII, 9, for the Conviction of Formalists, and the Awakening of Believers to Stand up Their Watch: Also the Way of the Hearts Working, and Pretious Remedies against Its Devices, Are Opened and Applyed with Other Things Observed Thereunto Belonging*. London: Printed for Samuel Crouch at the Corner-shop of Popes-head Alley on the right-hand next Cornhill, 1676.

Foster, Stephen. *The Long Argument: English Puritanism and the Shaping of New England Culture, 1570–1700*. Chapel Hill: University of North Carolina Press, 1991.

Freeman, Ray. *John Flavel: A Famous Dartmouth Puritan*. Paper 29. Dartmouth: Dartmouth History Research Group, 2001.

Galpine, John. "The Life of Mr. John Flavell." In *Mr. John Flavell's Remains: Being Two Sermons, Composed by That Reverend and Learned Divine*, A2r–A8r, by John Flavel. London: Printed for Tho. Cockerill, at the Three Legs in the Poultrey, 1691.

George, Timothy. *Theology of the Reformers*. Nashville: Broadman & Holman, 1988.

Gleason, Randall Craig. "John Calvin and John Owen: A Comparison of Their Teaching on Mortification." ThD diss., Dallas Theological Seminary, 1992.

Gordon, Bruce. *Calvin*. New Haven: Yale University Press, 2011.

Gore, Ralph J., Jr. "The Pursuit of Plainness: Rethinking the Puritan Regulative Principle of Worship." PhD diss., Westminster Theological Seminary, 1988.

Greaves, Richard L. *Glimpses of Glory: John Bunyan and English Dissent*. Stanford, Calif.: Stanford University Press, 2002.

Grell, Ole Peter, Jonathan I. Israel, and Nicholas Tyacke, eds. *From Persecution to Toleration: The Glorious Revolution and Religion in England*. Oxford: Oxford University Press, 1991.

Hall, David W., and Peter A. Lillback, eds. *Theological Guide to Calvin's Institutes*. Phillipsburg, N.J.: P&R, 2008.

Haller, William. *The Rise of Puritanism*. New York: Columbia University Press, 1938.

Hawkes, R. M. "The Logic of Assurance in English Puritan Theology." *Westminster Theological Journal* 52 (1990): 247–61.

Helm, Paul. *Calvin and the Calvinists*. Edinburgh: Banner of Truth, 1982.

Hill, Christopher. *The Century of Revolution, 1603–1714.* New York: W. W. Norton & Company, 1980.

———. *Puritanism and Revolution: Studies in Interpretation of the English Revolution of the Seventeenth Century.* New York: St. Martin's Press, 1997.

———. *Society and Puritanism in Pre-Revolutionary England.* Hampshire: Palgrave Macmillan, 1997.

Holbrook, Thomas. "Elaborated Labyrinth." PhD diss., University of Maryland, 1984.

Holley, Larry Jackson. "The Divines of the Westminster Assembly: A Study of Puritanism and Parliament." PhD diss., Yale University, 1979.

Horton, Robert Forman. *John Howe.* London: Methuen & Co., 1905.

Hume, David. *Dialogues Concerning Natural Religion.* Edited by Nelson Pike. New York: Bobbs-Merrill Co., 1970.

Johnson, Erik D. "Puritan Attitudes toward Providence and Pain: Suffering in England, 1647–1685." MCS thesis, Regent College, 1985.

Kamen, Henry. *The Rise of Toleration.* London: Littlehampton Book Services, 1967.

Kapic, Kelly M., and Randall C. Gleason, eds. *The Devoted Life: An Invitation to the Puritan Classics.* Downers Grove, Ill.: InterVarsity Press, 2004.

Kevan, Ernest F. *The Grace of Law: A Study in Puritan Theology.* Morgan, Pa.: Soli Deo Gloria, 1997.

Kistler, Don. *Thomas Watson: Pastor of St. Stephen's Walbook, London.* Morgan, Pa.: Soli Deo Gloria, 2004.

Knappen, M. M. *Tudor Puritanism.* Chicago: Chicago University Press, 1939.

Laurence, Anne, W. R. Owens, and Stuart Sim, eds. *John Bunyan and His England, 1628–1688.* London: Hambledon Press, 1990.

Lea, Thomas D. "The Hermeneutics of the Puritans." *Journal of the Evangelical Theological Society* 39, no. 2 (June 1996): 271–84.

Lee, Hansang. "Trinitarian Theology and Piety: The Attributes of God in the Thought of Stephen Charnock (1628–1680) and William Perkins (1558–1602). PhD diss., University of Edinburgh, 2009.

Letham, Robert. *The Westminster Assembly: Reading Its Theology in Historical Context.* Phillipsburg, N.J.: P&R, 2009.

Lewis, Peter. *The Genius of Puritanism*. Morgan, Pa.: Soli Deo Gloria, 1996.

Maddux, Clark. "Ramist Rationality, Covenant Theology, and the Poetics of Edward Taylor." PhD diss., Purdue University, 2001.

Matthews, A. G. *Calamy Revised, Being a Revision of Edmund Calamy's Account of the Ministers and Others Ejected and Silenced, 1660-2*. Oxford: The Clarendon Press, 1934.

McNeill, John T. *The History and Character of Calvinism*. New York: Oxford University Press, 1954.

M'Crie, Thomas. *Annals of English Presbytery*. London: James Nisbet & Co., 1872.

Menzies, John. *Flaveliana; Or, Selections from the Works of John Flavel with A Brief Sketch of His Life*. Edinburgh: John Menzies, 1859.

Miller, Perry. *The New England Mind*. Vol. 1, *The Seventeenth Century*. Cambridge: Harvard University Press, 1939.

Moorman, J. R. H. *A History of the Church in England*. 3rd ed. Harrisburg, Pa.: Morehouse Publishing, 1980.

Morrill, John, ed. *The Oxford Illustrated History of Tudor and Stuart Britain*. Oxford: Oxford University Press, 1996.

Muller, Richard A. *Post-Reformation Reformed Dogmatics*. 4 vols. Grand Rapids: Baker, 2003.

Mullett, Michael. *John Bunyan in Context*. Keele, U.K.: Keele University Press, 1996.

Murphy, Scott Thomas. "The Doctrine of Scripture in the Westminster Assembly." PhD diss., Drew University, 1984.

Murray, Iain H. "John Flavel." *Banner of Truth Magazine* 60 (September 1968): 3-5.

———. *The Puritan Hope: Revival and the Interpretation of Prophecy*. Edinburgh: Banner of Truth, 1971.

Nellen, H. J. M. "De zinspreuk 'In necessariis unitas, in non necessariis libertas, in utrisque caritas.'" *Nederlands archief voor kerkgeschidenis* 79, no. 1, 1999.

Noll, Mark A., David W. Bebbington, and George A. Rawlyk, eds. *Evangelicalism: Comparative Studies of Popular Protestantism in North America, the British Isles, and Beyond, 1700-1990*. Oxford: Oxford University Press, 1994.

Nuttall, Geoffrey F. *The Holy Spirit in Puritan Faith and Experience.* Chicago: University of Chicago Press, 1992.

Owen, John. Pneumatologia, *Or, A Discourse Concerning the Holy Spirit: Wherein an Account Is Given of His Name, Nature, Personality, Dispensation, Operations, and Effects; His Whole Work in the Old and New Creation Is Explained; The Doctrine Concerning It Vindicated from Oppositions and Reproaches.* London: 1674.

———. Pneumatologia, *Or, A Discourse Concerning the Holy Spirit.* Vol. 3 of *The Works of John Owen.* Edinburgh: Banner of Truth, 1965.

Packer, James I, ed. *Puritan Papers.* 5 vols. Phillipsburg, N.J.: P&R, 2000.

———. *A Quest for Godliness: The Puritan Vision of the Christian Life.* Wheaton, Ill.: Crossway Books, 1990.

———. "The Redemption and Restoration of Man in the Thought of Richard Baxter: A Study in Puritan Theology." DPhil diss., Oxford University, 1954.

Parker, Nathan. "Proselytism and Apocalypticism in England Before and After the Act of Toleration of 1689: The French Threat and a Lone Puritan." Paper delivered at the Cambridge Graduate Conference, Spring 2011.

Parker, T. H. L. *Calvin: A Biography.* Louisville: Westminster John Knox, 2007.

Peterkin, Alexander. *Records of the Kirk of Scotland, Containing the Acts and Proceedings of the General Assemblies, from the Year 1638 Downwards, As Authenticated by the Clerks of the Assembly; With Notes and Historical Illustrations.* Edinburgh: Printed by Peter Brown, 1843.

Plantinga, Alvin. *God, Freedom, and Evil.* Grand Rapids: Eerdmans, 1977.

Purkiss, Diane. *The English Civil War: Papists, Gentlewomen, Soldiers and Witchfinders in the Birth of Modern Britain.* New York: Basic Books, 2006.

Quick, John. Icones Sacrae Anglicanae *or The Lives and Deaths of Severall Eminent English Divines, Ministers of the Gospell, Pastors of Churches and Professors of Divinity in Our Owne and Foreigne Universitys.* 2 vols. Located in Dr. Williams Library, London, c. 1691.

———. Icones Sacrae Anglicanae *or The Lives and Deaths of Severall Eminent English Divines, Ministers of the Gospell, Pastors of*

Churches and Professors of Divinity in Our Owne and Foreigne Universitys. Located in Dr. William's Library, London, c. 1706.

Rogers, Richard. *Seven Treatises Containing Such Direction As Is Gathered out of the Holie Scriptures, Leading and Guiding to True Happines, Both in This Life, and in the Life to Come: And May Be Called the Practise of Christianitie. Profitable for All Such As Heartily Desire the Same: In the Which, More Particularly True Christians May Learne How to Leade a Godly and Comfortable Life Every Day. Penned by Richard Rogers, Preacher of the Word of God at Wethersfield in Essex.* London, 1603.

Sheils, W. J. *Persecution and Toleration.* London: Blackwell Publishers, 1984.

Sibbes, Richard. *The Bruised Reed.* Edinburgh: Banner of Truth, 1998.

———. *The Soul's Conflict with Itself.* In vol. 1 of *The Complete Works of Richard Sibbes.* Edited by Alexander Balloch Grosart. Edinburgh: James Nichol, 1862.

Siekawitch, Larry Daniel. "Stephen Charnock's Doctrine of the Knowledge of God: A Case Study of the Balance of Head and Heart in Restoration Puritanism." PhD diss., University of Wales, Bangor, 2007.

Spurr, John. *English Puritanism, 1603–1689.* London: Macmillan Press, 1998.

———. *The Post-Reformation: Religion, Politics and Society in Britain, 1603–1714.* Harlow, UK: Pearson Education Ltd., 2006.

Stephensen, Sally Ann. "The Ministerial and Theological Purposes of Jonathan Edwards' Thought: A Study in Source and Context." PhD diss., University of Pennsylvania, 1983.

Thompson, Ann. *The Art of Suffering and the Impact of Seventeenth-Century Anti-Providential Thought.* Burlington, Vt.: Ashgate, 2003.

Tindall, William York. *John Bunyan: Mechanic Preacher.* New York: Columbia University Press, 1934.

Toon, Peter, ed. *Puritans and Calvinism.* Swengel, Pa.: Reiner Publications, 1973.

———. *Puritans, the Millennium and the Future of Israel: Puritan Eschatology 1600 to 1660.* Cambridge: James Clarke & Co., 1970.

VanderMolen, Ronald J. "Providence as Mystery, Providence as Revelation: Puritan and Anglican Modifications of John Calvin's Doctrine of Providence." *Church History* 47, no. 1 (March 1978): 27–47.

Van Dixhoorn, Chad B., ed. *The Minutes and Papers of the Westminster Assembly, 1643–1653.* 5 vols. Oxford: Oxford University Press, 2012.

———. "Reforming the Reformation: Theological Debate at the Westminster Assembly, 1642–1652." PhD diss., University of Cambridge, 2004.

Vickers, Douglas. Review of *The Works of John Flavel*. *Westminster Theological Journal* 32, no. 1 (November 1969–May 1970): 92–96.

Von Rohr, John. *The Covenant of Grace in Puritan Thought.* Eugene, Ore.: Wipf & Stock, 2010.

Vose, Godfrey Noel. "Profile of a Puritan: John Owen." PhD diss., State University of Iowa, 1963.

Wallace, Dewey D. "John Flavel." In *Puritans and Puritanism in Europe and America.* Edited by Francis J. Bremer and Tom Webster. Santa Barbara, Calif.: ABC-CLIO, 2006.

———. "The Life and Thought of John Owen to 1660: A Study of the Significance of Calvinist Theology in English Puritanism." PhD diss., Princeton University, 1965.

———. *Puritans and Predestination: Grace in English Protestant Theology, 1525–1695.* Eugene, Ore.: Wipf & Stock, 1982.

Walsham, Alexandra. *Charitable Hatred: Tolerance and Intolerance in England, 1500–1700.* Manchester: Manchester University Press, 2006.

———. *Providence in Early Modern England.* Oxford: Oxford University Press, 1999.

Warfield, Benjamin B. *The Westminster Assembly and Its Work.* In vol. 6 of *The Works of Benjamin B. Warfield.* New York: Oxford University Press, 1932. Reprint, Grand Rapids: Baker, 2003.

Watson, Thomas. *Autarkeia; Or, The Art of Divine Contentment.* Printed by T. R. & E. M. for Ralph Smith at the signe of the Bible in Cornhil, near the Royall Exchange, 1653.

———. *A Body of Practical Divinity: Consisting of Sermons on the Lesser Catechism.* London: Printed for Thomas Parkhurst, 1692.

Watts, Michael R. *The Dissenters*. Oxford: Clarendon Press, 1978.

Whiting, C. E., ed. *Studies in English Puritanism from the Restoration to the Revolution, 1660–1688*. New York: The Macmillan Company, 1931.

Williams, J. B. *The Lives of Philip and Matthew Henry*. Edinburgh: Banner of Truth, 1974.

Wilson, Walter. *The History and Antiquities of Dissenting Churches and Meeting Houses, in London, Westminster, and Southwark; Including the Lives of Their Ministers, from the Rise of Nonconformity to the Present Time*. 4 vols. London: Printed for the Author; Sold by W. Button and Son, Paternoster Row, 1808.

Windeatt, Edward. "John Flavell: A Notable Dartmouth Puritan and His Bibliography." In *Report and Transactions of the Devonshire Association for the Advancement of Science, Literature, and Art*. Vol. 43. Plymouth: W. Brendon and Son, 1911.

Wong, David Wai-Sing. "The Covenant Theology of John Owen." PhD diss., Westminster Theological Seminary, 1998.

———. "John Owen on the Suffering of Christ and the Suffering of the Church." ThM thesis, Westminster Theological Seminary, 1990.

Wood, Anthony á. Athenæ Oxonienses: *An Exact History of All the Writers and Bishops Who Have Had Their Education in the University of Oxford*. Vol. 4. New York: Lackington, Hughes, Harding, et al., 1820.

Woodhouse, A. S. P. *Puritanism and Liberty*. London: Macmillan, 1938.

Yuille, Stephen J. *The Inner Sanctum of Puritan Piety: John Flavel's Doctrine of Mystical Union with Christ*. Grand Rapids: Reformation Heritage Books, 2007.

Index

Act of Uniformity, 4
Adam, 16–18
addiction, 24
adoption
    Bunyan on, 109
    and Holy Spirit, 119–20
    and providence, 46
affections
    and assurance, 116–17
    development of, 81
    sanctification of, 74, 77–78
affliction
    and assurance, 112
    Bunyan on, 109
    and evil, 52
    and exposure of sin, 62–63
    improving of, 102–5
    as momentary, 135–38
    and providence, 48
    rod of, 126
    suffering of, 21
    and vanity, 74–75
    as warning, 60
Allestree, Richard, 15
all-sufficiency (of God), 72–73
Arminianism, 8
assurance, 77, 95–99, 133
    and adoption, 119–20
    and Bible, 127–28
    grounds for, 120–26
    and Holy Spirit, 115–17

    and means or grace, 126–27
    and obedience, 131–32
    and prayer, 128–30
    quest for, 107–11
    and sacraments, 130–31
    and suffering, 111–15
Augustine, 92
authority (of God), 37–38

Baxter, Richard, 3, 4
    Chang on, 8
    and Flavel, 5, 38–39
Beeke, Joel R.
    on assurance, 108n2, 109–11, 133
    on *Divine Conduct*, 32
    on Holy Spirit, 115
Bible
    and assurance, 127–28
    and fellowship with God, 82–83
    on prayer, 85
    and providence, 36–37
    and suffering, 10
blessings, 30
Boland, Michael, 33
Bremer, Francis, 32
Bromsgrove, Worcesterchire, 3
Bunyan, John, 3
    on assurance, 109
    on suffering, 19
burning in effigy, 5
Burroughs, Jeremiah, 14

Calvin, John
   Chang on, 7–8
   on Lord's Supper, 86
   on secondary causes, 38–39
Calvinism, 7–8
chance, 44, 48, 50
Chang, Kwai Sing, 3n4, 7–9, 38, 42
Charles II, 4
church
   purity of, 79–80
   sanctification of, 67–68
   suffering of, 92
Church of England, 4
clock illustration, 40n45
comfort
   and assurance, 111–15, 130–31
   from Bible, 127–28
   and Lord's Supper, 87, 88
   nature of, 75–77
   and prayer, 128–30
   and providence, 46–47
common grace, 45
complaint, 85–86, 100
condemnation
   quest for, 97–99
   and suffering, 17
contentment, 10–11
conviction, 81n121
covenant of grace
   and assurance, 111, 120–24
   and Lord's Supper, 86
covenant of works, 121
Cragg, Gerald, 16
creation
   curse on, 17
   sufficiency of, 75, 76
curse
   and Christ's death, 87
   on creation, 17
   suffering as, 18

death, 4, 17, 138–39
   of Christ, 50, 92–94
   of Christian, 119
Deckard, Mark, 32–33
decree
   and evil, 53
   and sovereignty of God, 35–38, 43–44
   and suffering, 18, 20
deism, 9, 38–42
depravity, 17
depression, 30
despair, 20, 27, 77
despondency, 81n121
determinism, 41
Devon, 4
discipline, 60, 70
discouragement, 27
divine sovereignty. *See* sovereignty of God
doubt, 79. *See also* assurance
Downs, Ann. *See* Flavel, Ann
duty, 103–4

effectual calling, 121
elect, 19
   and communion with Christ, 91–94
   and providence, 46
   sin of, 61–62
   suffering of, 50, 58–61, 100–101
election, 120–24
Elys, Edmund, 5
encouragement, 81n121
England, 5
eternity, 43, 135–42
evil
   and sovereignty of God, 51–55
   and suffering, 14–15, 18–19

faith, 67, 99–100
   and assurance, 110, 111–15
   and comfort, 77
   and communion with Christ, 93–94

and depression, 30
and Holy Spirit, 116, 117–19
and Lord's Supper, 86–87
and prayer, 129
and sacraments, 130
signs of, 127
and suffering, 78–80, 100–101, 103
and Word of God, 83
faithfulness, 70, 90
fall of Adam, 16–18
family, 24
fatalism, 41
fear, 77, 79. *See also* assurance
Ferguson, Sinclair, 32
Five Mile Act, 4
Flavel, Ann, 4
Flavel, Elizabeth, 4
Flavel, Jane, 4
Flavel, John, 1–4
    Chang on, 7–9
    Divine Conduct, 32–34
    influence of, 4–5
    interpretations of, 6–7
    on sovereignty of God, 35–38
    Thompson on, 9–11
    works of, 5–6
fruit
    of Holy Spirit, 67–68
    of sin, 17–18

Galpine, John, 5
glory of God, 34, 53, 57–59
    display of, 68–73, 90
    and good works, 67
God. *See also* glory of God; Holy Spirit; sovereignty of God; will of God
    attributes of, 37, 68–73
    and comfort, 75–77
    and covenant of grace, 123
    decrees of, 43–44
    delight in, 27
    and evil, 53
    fellowship with, 80–82
    and happiness, 66–67
    prayer to, 83–86
    providence of, 44–48
    rod of, 48, 126
    and Satan, 25, 28–30
    spiritual suffering, 29–30
    and suffering, 18
    Word of, 82–83
godliness, 66–68, 78
good
    of elect, 59
    and evil, 53
    God as, 19, 71
    suffering as, 29
    works, 67
Goodwin, John, 8
governance, 45
grace
    and adoption, 120
    and decree, 43
    display of, 71
    faith as, 113
    and fall into sin, 16
    and Holy Spirit, 118
    improving of, 103, 131
    means of, 111, 126–27
    and union with Christ, 93
Great Fire of London (1666), 14
Great Plague (1665), 14
grief, 20
guilt
    consciousness of, 80
    and covenant of grace, 124
    as spiritual suffering, 27

happiness
    as eternal, 137
    of heaven, 139–41
    source of, 75, 77
    and suffering, 66–67
Hawkes, R. M., 111

healing, 136
heart, 132
heaven
   hope of, 139–41
   seal of, 118, 120
heavenly-mindedness, 67, 73–74, 77–78
hell, 141
holiness
   and evil, 53
   and providence, 46
Holy Spirit
   and adoption, 119–20
   and assurance, 110, 115–17
   and faith, 94
   fruit of, 67–68
   and prayer, 85
   sealing work of, 117–19
   and Word of God, 45
   and union with Christ, 125
hope, 118, 138–41
Houlbrooke, Ralph
   on life, 139–40
   on prayer, 84
Howe, John, 4, 8
humanity
   responsibility of, 41
   and Satan, 25
humility, 67, 101–2
hypocrisy, 78–80

idolatry
   and comfort, 76
   and suffering, 64–65
   temptation to, 26
image of God, 17
immutability, 43, 72
instruction, 81n121
intermediate state, 138–39

jealousy, 73
Jesus Christ
   and affliction, 52

communion with, 91–94
   and Holy Spirit, 116
   and Lord's Supper, 86–88
   love of, 111
   receiving of, 119–20
   return of, 138–39
   and Satan, 25
   suffering for, 28
   suffering of, 49, 60
   union with, 124–26
joy
   and assurance, 112, 114
   and Christ's suffering, 92
   of elect, 34
   of heaven, 139–41
   and Lord's Supper, 87, 88
   source of, 75, 77
   and suffering, 58, 72, 101
judgment, 141
   sign of, 89, 90–91
   of wicked, 59–61
justice, 72
justification, 99–100, 113–14

Kelly, James William, 3n4
Kidder, Richard, 14

Lewis, Peter, 29
life, 139–41
Lord's Supper
   and assurance, 130–31
   and fellowship with God, 86–88
love
   and affliction, 52, 60
   assurance of, 111
   display of, 70–71
   and election, 122
   sincerity of, 79
   of world, 73–74
lust, 62

Manton, Thomas, 4
Marshall, William, 14n4

Martyrdom, 24, 118–19
means of grace, 111, 126–27
mercy, 71
ministers, 29, 42
Morris, Elizabeth. *See* Flavel, Elizabeth
mortification, 62, 64–66
Murray, Iain, 138, 140
mystery, 33–34

natural causes, 9–10, 40–42
nature, 9–10
New England, 5

obedience, 131–32
omnipotence, 35, 37, 43
omniscience, 35, 43, 46
original sin, 16–17, 19–20, 25
Owen, John, 3
    on assurance, 108–9
    Chang on, 7–8
    and Flavel, 5, 38–39
Oxford, University of, 4

pain, 21. *See also* suffering
paradise, 17, 138
patience, 73, 96, 141
Paul, 92
peace, 46
Perkins, William, 84
persecution, 4, 14, 15–16
    benefits of, 68
    and external suffering, 21
perseverance, 125
pleasure
    danger of, 132
    and suffering, 27–28, 64–65, 74–75
polemics, 99
poverty, 14
practical syllogism, 119–20
prayer
    and assurance, 128–30

    and fellowship with God, 83–86
    and providence, 46
    as response to suffering, 101
preaching, 131
preservation, 45
pride, 27, 65
problem of evil. *See* evil
promises, 44, 84
    and Holy Spirit, 118
    and Lord's Supper, 86
prosperity, 64, 79–80
providence
    and comfort, 76
    Flavel on, 10
    improving of, 104
    as mystery, 33–34
    Puritans on, 31–32
    and secondary causes, 41–42
    and sovereignty of God, 35–38, 44–47
    submission to, 101–2
    and suffering, 18, 29, 97–99
    Thompson on, 11
Puritans
    on assurance, 107–11
    Chang on, 7–8
    covenant theology of, 121n66
    and deism, 39
    on life, 139–40
    on prayer, 84
    on suffering, 57, 95–99
    as theologians, 1–3
    Thompson on, 10
reconciliation, 68
redemption, 124
religion, 28
restoration, 16
resurrection, 138–39
revelation, 35–37
righteousness
    display of, 72
    Jesus as, 124
    and suffering, 58, 68

Rogers, Richard, 13
Roman Catholicism, 111n17

sacraments, 130–31. *See also* Lord's Supper
Salisbury, 4
salvation, 43. *See also* assurance
sanctification
   of affections, 74
   of affliction, 52, 60–61
   and Bible, 127
   and election, 121
   Jesus as, 124
   negative, 61–66
   positive, 66–68
   as sealing, 117
Satan, 24–30
Scripture. *See* Bible
secondary causes, 9–10, 38–42
security, 46
Sibbes, Richard, 3
   on deism, 39
   on Satan, 24
sin
   and affliction, 52, 53
   and Bible, 82
   and covenant of grace, 124
   deterring of, 63–64
   exposure of, 62–63
   mortification, 64–66
   Satan's use of, 26–27
   and spiritual suffering, 24
   and suffering, 16–20, 58, 61–62
sincerity, 79–80
song, 101
sorrow
   and comfort, 77
   as response to suffering, 100
   as spiritual suffering, 27
   as suffering, 20, 21–22
sovereignty of God
   and decree, 35–38, 43–44
   display of, 71–72
   and evil, 51–55
   Flavel on, 35–38
   and prayer, 83–86, 129
   and providence, 44–47
   Puritans on, 31–32
   and secondary causes, 41–42
   and suffering, 19–20, 47–51, 135–36
   Thompson on, 9–11
Spurr, John
   on persecution, 16
   on providence, 31
submission, 101–2
suffering
   benefits of, 10
   cessation of, 135–42
   and divine attributes, 68–73
   and evil, 52
   external, 20–21
   of Flavel, 3–4
   improving of, 102–5
   internal, 21–23
   of Jesus, 49, 60, 91–94
   kinds of, 20
   origin of, 16–20
   purposes of, 57–61
   response to, 95–99
   and sanctification, 61–68
   and sin, 61–62
   and sovereignty of God, 19–20, 47–51
   spiritual, 23–30
   in Stuart England, 14–16
   theology of, 1, 11–12
   Thompson on, 9–11
   types of, 13
   as witness to world, 88–91
   and Word of God, 82–83
suicide, 24

temptation
   affliction, 65
   Satan's use of, 25–26

thanksgiving, 101
theodicy, 51
theology, 7–9, 11–12
Thompson, Ann, 42, 100, 103
   and deism, 39–40
   on Flavel, 9–11
   on suffering, 95–99
   tree of knowledge of good and evil, 16
   tree of life, 17
   truth, 36–37

unbelief, 100

vanity, 74–75
Von Rohr, John, 121n66

Wallace, Dewey D., Jr., 3n4
Walsham, Alexandra
   on assurance, 89
   on deism, 39
   on providence, 31–32
   on sovereignty of God, 35
   on suffering, 57
Watson, Thomas, 3, 4
   on assurance, 108
   on deism, 39
   on Satan, 24
Westminster Confession of Faith
   on assurance, 109–11, 133
   and Flavel, 8–9
Westminster Shorter Catechism, 43, 44

   Flavel on, 8–9, 128
   on Holy Spirit, 115–16
   Watson on, 108
wicked, 19, 59–61
will of God
   and evil, 53
   and prayer, 85
   and sovereignty, 37–38
   submission to, 101–2
wisdom
   display of, 69–70
   of God, 43
   Jesus as, 124
   and providence, 46
witness, 88–91
Wood, Anthony á, 4–5
Word of God
   and fellowship with God, 82–83
   and Holy Spirit, 45
   and providence, 36–37
world, 88–91
worldliness
   and affliction, 62
   and suffering, 73–75
worship, 71
wrath
   and affliction, 60–61
   and Christ's death, 87
   and suffering, 17, 48

Yuille, J. Stephen
   on Flavel's birth, 3n4
   on perseverance, 125